AF755586

GYĀRASPUR
A HERITAGE OF EXCELLENCE

GYĀRASPUR
A HERITAGE OF EXCELLENCE

DEV RAJ BIRDI

1991

Sharada Prakashan

DELHI-110052

First Published 1991

© Dev Raj Birdi (b. 1955-)

ISBN : 81-85320-12-8

SHARADA ₹ 750/-

Published by
SHARADA PRAKASHAN
E-239, Shastri Nagar, Delhi-110052.
Ph. 516539

Typeset by
Neographics, 2/7, Ansari Road, New Delhi-110002

Printed at
Raj Press, R-3, Inderpuri, New Delhi-110012

To

MY BEST CRITIC

CONTENTS

PREFACE

Being an administrator I always kept out of my dictionary the terms like delicacy, tenderness, sensuousness and so on. As a routine tour to the villages I saw some monuments, idols and some decorative stone slabs and gazed at them but I paid no attention. But to my ease, sometime, I felt something deep into my heart, as these ancient relics wanted to reveal some mystery that I could not understand.

My district has a museum which, now I can say, has a beautiful collection of sculptures, excavated material, coins and so many things alike, belonging to bygone heydays that the district had enjoyed. In the course of repeated visits to the museum, these too, stamped upon me an impression and evoked the same feeling.

While working on administration I had to consult the history part which by virtue of curiosity dragged me out for a long period. Meanwhile I visited Gyāraspur, the picturesque landscaping together with imposing monuments startled me with a fierce urge to probe into the books to know something about as to what they have to convey. I saw several books, administrative reports but could not find out anything more than scanty and occasional notes and the copies made thereof by successive authors. This led me to build up an idea of conveying something new, the truth, to the public and to the art historians, which resulted into the present work.

During the course of my studies for this book I found almost a stereotyped approach made by various writers to explain the art, reasoning it by political history and witnessing by Purāṇic and Sanskrit literature references and saying something about expressions displayed. I thought of philosophy, psychology, eco-social environment that acted mystically behind this ripe creation. I have tried to make an approach with this idea without knowing the reaction.

In fact, it is for Mr. K.K. Chakravarty, Commissioner, Archaeology and Museums, Madhya Pradesh, Bhopal who brought me into the domain of archaeology and encouraged me to take up the study of ancient monuments and sculptures.

To Mr. Deepak Mahashabde, and Dr. Prakashendra Mathur, I am indebted for their incessant help in identification of sculptures and for digging out the references.

My thanks are due to Mr. Ashok Maheshwari, who provided me the photographs.I am specially obliged to Mr. R.V. Joshi and Mr. R.D. Parashar for their help in typing the manuscript.

The main credit for this book must go to Mr. B.L. Bansal of M/s Sharada Prakashan, Delhi who suggested to me to write this book. He has also seen the book through the Press with his utmost efficiency.

Lastly I must thank my wife Sharoo for her constant inspiration and encouragement.

14 January 1991 DEV RAJ BIRDI
Makar Sankranti
VIDIŚĀ.

ABBREVIATIONS

Anc.	-	Ancient.
ASI, or A.S.I.	-	Archaeological Survey of India.
AS	-	Archaeological Survey.
ASR	-	Archaeological Survey Reports.
ASIR	-	Archaeological Survey of India : A Review.
D.G.	-	District Gazetteers.
EI	-	Epigraphia Indica.
IA	-	Indian Antiquary.
IHQ	-	Indian Historical Quarterly.
JASI	-	Journal of Asiatic Society of India.
JBORS	-	Journal of the Bihar and Orissa Research Society.
RV	-	Ṛgveda.

I

Introduction

Since time immemorial the valleys of Betwa and Bes have cradled great centres of culture and civilisation that have left their marks in history of ancient India. Gyāraspur lies in a george of low steep hills as a cozy and snug patch of habitation is approachable through the old highway to the Sagar at about 38.4 Km. from Vidiśā. The scattered relics and the ruins of temples in and around the village yelling their prosperity and heydays they enjoyed in early medieval time. The ruins indicate the place has patronaged Buddhism, Śaivism, Vaiṣṇavism and Jainism with secular spirit without any controversy.

The name of Gyāraspur is believed to have derived from a big monthly auspicious fair organised on every Gyāras—the eleventh day of Hindu month. Perhaps it may also be possible that it might have been a complex of eleven small villages as the tradition expounds the name of Daśapur (modern Mandsaur) or Varāhakheḍi alias Bārākhéḍi in Raisen District are after the complex of ten and twelve villages.

The picturesque landscaping and romantic appearance of geographical undulating ups and downs provided a favourable atmosphere to hold on the religious congregations, deep meditation and concentration and thinking together with the regulations of modest social community. Being an important place of culture by the side of main highway running from north to south—'from Uttarāpatha to Dakṣiṇāpatha', it has imbibed various regional features. Swollen like an island midst the valley of Vindhya with the humus of black cotton soil mixed with alluvian silt and good water sources provided the fair opportunity for agricultural activities. The ancient relics and monuments such as Mālādevī temple, Hindola Toraṇ, Bajramaṭh, Aṭha Khambā, Buddhist stūpas, Katārmal Bhairav and world renowned sculpture of celestial nymph Śālabhañjikā boast about the architectural and art splendour of Gyāraspur. Mr. A. Cunningham in the year 1871-72 visited the monuments of Gyāraspur and his report has included the details.[1] It is obvious that the image of Jain Tīrthaṅkara studded on the śikhara of Bajramaṭh, the figure of goddess at the lalāṭa-biṃba of Mālādevī Mahāmaṇḍapa entrance door and the Hindola Toraṇ misled Mr. Cunningham to conclude that the Bajramaṭh was originally a Buddhist temple and the Mālādevī was dedicated to some Hindu goddess. Likewise the Hindola Toraṇ is a prestigious entrance to the Buddhist stūpa. He also misled to identify the lofty Jain Tīrthaṅkaras images in all the shrines of Bajramaṭh as the images of Buddha. Mr. M.B. Garde, the Superintendent of Archaeology in Scindia State rightly identified the Bajramaṭh sculptures but he accepted the Cunningham report saying the Mālādevī temple was originally dedicated to some Hindu goddess.[2] The later scholars such as Dr. D.R. Patil,[3] Mr. M.D. Khare[4] never tried to find out the truth except blindly followed their predecessors.

In the year 1933-35 Shri M.B. Garde, undertook the restoration and clearance of Hindola Toraṇ, Mālādevī and the Bajramaṭh among them he focussed his attention on the restoration of Mālādevī temple. While removing the debris at Hindola Toraṇ in 1933 he recovered a torso of a lady without head with mutilated hands and legs broken from knees. The clearance of successive years became a boon to his discoveries as he picked up a small head and fortunately that fitted to the torso.[5] This total idol with fascinating smile, he identified as 'Śālabhañjikā' or the 'Gyāraspur lady' which is now a shining star of celestial globe of the art approached the zenith during the early period. After the formation of Madhya Bharat and then the State of Madhya Pradesh in 1956 the monuments of Gyāraspur are taken care of by the Archaeological Survey of India.

Occasional survey have yielded some stone implements belonging to early stone age to mesolithic period.

The Besnagar excavations have yielded sufficient material to frame-up an idea about the chalcolithic culture and the successive Aryan influence over the land.

After 1956 no attempts have been made so far to find out the reasoning or the logic behind the erection of these monuments, which, in fact, are the best testimonials to judge the artistic splendour, the social and religious beliefs in and around Gyāraspur during medieval period.

References

1. Cunningham, A., *Archaeological Survey Reports*, 1871-72, Vol. VII, p. 90.
2. *Annual Administrative Reports, Gwalior State,* 1932-33, p. 4.
3. Patil, D.R., *Cultural Heritage of Madhya Bharat*, p. 107.
4. Khare, M.D., *Vidiśā* (Hindi), p. 182.
5. It is really very fateful regarding the artistic valuation of this image that upto 1962, this has been merely identified as the woman in the catalogue to the sculptures of Gwalior Museum. S. No. 2 of Room No. 33, p. 14 giving a very shallow description as 'Standing with an ornamental head-dress and a hood behind, wears three necklaces, a pendent

of the lowest coming to the waist and Vṛkṣikā' by S.K. Dixit, *A Guide to Gwalior Museum.* Mr. Dixit has not included this in his catalogue, he did only printed the photograph on back of the booklet.

II

Prologue—Historical Profile

The first stroke of hammer on flake was a break into the dawn of civilisation in the valleys of Betwa and Bes competing to the human activities in other parts of Vindhyan ranges in early stone age. The recovery of palaeolithic tools, the hand axes, cleavers, scrapers, the chalcolithic tools and the black painted red and black, and red ware evidently indicate towards the nomadic habitation in the area.[1] Precisely the history of Vidiśā or the Daśārṇa Janapada, out of sixteen Mahājanapada in 6th century B.C. is the history of Gyāraspur and its vicinity.

The epics and purāṇas speak much about the Daśārṇa and Vidiśā, in particular, as it was located on main national highway running from Uttarāpatha to Dakṣiṇāpatha or to say from Mathurā, Padmāvati, Vidiśā onwards to Bhṛgukachchha and Shurparak (Sopara) in Maharashtra.[2] These two routes, by now, have been adopted by the Central Railway. The southern expedition led by Bhīma and Sahadeva tells about the defeat of the king of Daśārṇa Janapada and then devastating the local tribes of Korkus (near the Bhīm Baithakā in Raisen district), they crossed Narmada and conquered the Chedi Janapada.[3] Similarly the Mahābhārata also speaks about the birth of Karṇa episode in which his mother Kunti floats the infant in Dhasān river of Daśārṇa region.

The Brahmanical, Buddhist and Jain texts refer to the various names of Vidiśā as Vesanagar, Besnagar, Bedis. We do find the name Bedis engraved on the tribal coins.[4] A few of them have been picked up during the excavation at Besnagar. In Bāveru Jātaka and Chaṇḍa Pradyota and Jīvaka episode makes mention of Vidiśā alongwith Gonaddha, Ujjain and Mahishmati.[5]

The Sanskrit literatures, dramatics and poetry narrate the prosperous life in Vidiśā and it's importance as a main trade centre exporting the wine, jewels, essences and luxurious textiles, ivory and agricultural and forest products through Ujjain to Soparā and Bharoch[6] as these were the main seaports of the country. Kālidāsa's romantic narrations in the Meghadūta envy the social fanaticism and hilaric atmosphere of the time.[7]

The history which can be supported by the historical relics, began with the sovereignty of Mauryas over the land as we learn from Dīpavaṃśa and Mahāvaṃśa that the Mauryan ruler Bindusāra, the father of Aśoka, appointed him as viceroy of Vidiśā, who during his stay married the daughter of a banker.[8] Her son Mahendra and daughter Saṅghmitrā who went upto Ceylon as the religious Ambassadors of their father. The excavation conducted in 1912 to 1919 by Sir John Marshall, Archaeological Survey of India at Sanchi revealed the remains of a monastery which was supposed to be a royal palace for the queen Devi, the wife of Aśoka. Bṛhadratha, the last of the Mauryan dynasty was turned down by his commander of army, Puṣyamitra Śuṅga, in 187 B.C. had been monitored by Patañjali who was doing sacrifices for the Puṣyamitra's success. This rebel was the result of fiercely dominating Buddhist religion making the young ones, the monk and the nuns, causing the adulteration in the sangh. At the same time the royal army was enamoured by the doctrine of Buddhism roaming throughout the domain with Buddhist emblem. Sometime during this transition Vidiśā must have emerged as an independent city state for a short while. This can be justified by the discovery of the copper coin bearing upon the three Brāhmi letters Vediśa or Veddasa characteristically analogous to that of Aśokan Brāhmi of 3rd-2nd century B.C. Puṣyamitra tried to recapture the original state of Vidiśā by marrying his son Agnimitra to princess Mālavikā of Vidarbha Desh. This romantic episode narrating the love affairs of Agnimitra and Mālavikā is beautifully elaborated by Kālidāsa in *Mālavikāgnimitram*—an unparalleled creation of the time. Like Aśoka, Agnimitra, too, served his father as the Viceroy of Vidiśā. It was the time when the magnificent and prestigeous gateways of Sanchi Mahāstūpa were erected with the visualisation of Jatak stories, where the glimpses of society, custom and belief are still throbbing. The Besnagar pillar inscription at Vidiśā tells about the conversion of Greek Ambassador Heliodorus, son of Dion, to the Bhāgavata faith and the erection of Garuḍaḍhvaja in front of eliptical Viṣṇu temple. And it is a good example of the prevalence of Bhāgavata cult in the region. Although the Purāṇas speak about the successor of Agnimitra but none can be equated by any archaeological evidences except Jyéṣṭhamitra who's a very few coins have been discovered.[9]

'The history repeats itself', the phrase can be justified by the incident occurred in 82 B.C., when the last Śuṅga king Devabhūti,[10] who was overfond of women's company, was murdered at the instance of his minister Vāsudeva, a Kaṇva Brāhmaṇa. Thus usurping the Magadha throne Vāsudeva could not get a stronghold on the administration and the Kaṇvas had to left the throne only after 45 years to the Śatavāhanas.[11]

The period from 1st century B.C. to 2nd century A.D. can be considered of unrest as the prolonged war between the western Kṣatrapas of north-west and Śātavāhanas of the south. This has tumbled the stability and the tranquillity, as both the houses were trying to extend their empires and Vidiśā as, north-eastern part of the Śātavāhana empire, had to loose its elegance and prosperity a bit. The Purāṇas state that Śātakarṇi had overcome the throne of Malwa in 72 B.C. but he had to hand it over to western Kṣatrapas. The coins unearthed in Vidiśā excavations belong to Kṣaharāta and Kardamaka shows that the two houses of the dynasty served as the Viceroys. The Bhūmaka and the Nahpāna could sustained the stability by extending the boundaries of empires upto Ajmer in the north and Nāsik and Poona in the south. The Nāsik and Kārlā inscription of Uśavdutta refers the extensive boundaries of empire undertaking the Malwa, Narmada valley, Kokan and the western part of Vidiśā and the whole Maharashtra. But Gautamiputra Śātakarṇi killing his northern opponent took into his possession the Saurāṣṭra, Anūpa, Ākara (Eastern Malwa) and Avanti (Western Malwa) but the Junagarh rock inscriptions of Rudradāman of 150 A.D. state that Gautamiputra Śātakarṇi had to loose the hold on Malwa to Scythian rulers known as Kardamaka. What the political activities had been, the artists unaware of this political ups and downs, was engrossed in the art creation as it is evident from the inscriptions on the southern gate of Sanchi, that a foreman of artisans Ānand donated the architraves of the gate in the Śātavāhana realm mentioning the name Śātakarṇi. Ptolemy refers about the Ujjain as the capital of Chaṣṭana. It is presumed that the enmity between the Rudradāman and Śātakarṇi could only be settled by matrimonial alliance marrying the daughter of Rudradāman to the son of Gautamiputra Śātakarṇi. The bridegroom was the brother of Vasiṣṭhīputra Pulumāvi, whose coins are of archaeological importance.

The excavation at Besnagar yielded a few copper coins bearing the name of Nāga rulers justifying the Purāṇic references. Dr. H.V. Trivedi while publishing the coins of Vṛṣanāga concluded that he was a Nāga prince who originated the Nāga house of Pawaya establishing himself at Vidiśā in the later half of 2nd century A.D.[12] Accepting the view of Dr. A.S. Altekar, Dr. Trivedi further says that the recovery of Vṛṣanāga coins from Vidiśā prove the identical principality in the region and the term Vṛṣas as referred by Purāṇas should be interpreted as Nṛpaḥ and not the Bull as some of the scholars have understood, neither it is a scribble error. Dr. H.V. Trivedi confirmed this hypothesis through his findings of several Vṛṣanāga coins at Pawaya the ancient Padmāvatī which fountained the prosperity under Nāga realm. The offshoots of the dynasty swayed upto Padmāvatī, Kāntipurī and Mathurā as the separate branches.[13] Although Nāga could not sustained their hold on Vidiśā but for centuries together theirs aureole enlightened the minds of society who never forgot to carve out the image of Balarāma, an incarnation of Śeṣanāga with the ten incarnation of Viṣṇu in medieval period.

The Purāṇic references expressed the probability of Vākāṭaka rule over some parts of the district Vidiśā elaborating Vindyaśakti (C. A.D. 255-275), as the founder of the dynasty who enlarging his patrimony and extending the limits across the Vindhya upto some portion of Malwa. Dr. R.C. Majumdar and Dr. A.S. Altekar believe that this may perhaps be the reason for the Purāṇic explanation that the Vindyaśakti as a ruler of Vidiśā.[14]

The Allahabad pillar inscription of Samudragupta, a marvellous Sanskrit composition by Hariṣeṇa in

Champu style of poetry (an admixure of prose and poetry) praises the deeds of Samudragupta and it clearly mentions the name of two Nāga rulers Gaṇpati Nāga and Nāgasena whom the Samudragupta vanquished in his southern expeditions.[15] He maintained the friendly relations with Nāga rulers by marrying his son, Chandragupta II with Kubernāgā, the Nāga princess. The Prayāga Praśasti also mentions the name of some tribes which were subdued by Samudragupta—the Sanakānikas and Kākas which are still inhabiting the Vidiśā district and the name of Kākapur is after the Kāka tribes.[16] This tribe has enjoyed the sovereignty in 3rd century B.C. and contributed a lot in building up the Sanchi Stūpas as the name of hill was termed Kaknadvot. Skandagupta seems to have maintained the friendly relations with Nāga appointing Sarva Nāga as a provincial Governor of the district in Ganga-Yamuna Doab.

Chandragupta has been eulogised as almighty unhampered ruler of the dynasty. The Sanchi inscription reads "*Mahārājādhirāja Śrī Chandraguptasya Devarāja iti priyanāmaḥ*"[17] and some other inscriptions make mention of his another name as Devaśrī. His undisputed sovereignty in Malwa is established by two epigraphs in the caves of Udaigiri Hills, one records the gift made by his feudatory Mahārāja Sankānika and another the excavation of a cave by his Minister Vīrasena. The Udaigiri inscription is composed by Vīrasena who was the royal poet with equal command on Jurisprudence, Grammar and Politics. His winsome knowledge is praised in the inscription as follows :

> *'Śabdārtha-nyāya-lokeśa kaviḥ Pāṭaliputrakaḥ*
> *Kautsāsav iti khyāto Vīrsaenaḥ Kulākhkhyayā'*
>
> (Udaigiri Cave Ins. Verse 4)

Chandragupta stayed long in Malwa in order to eradicate the Śaka ruler Rudradāman III and married Dhruvasvāminī, the wife of his elder brother Ramagupta. He assumed the title of Vikramāditya after his unequitable victory towards the Śaka rulers. Some scholars and art critics are of opinion that the massive Nṛvarāha of Udaigiri is the representation of Chandragupta who by expelling the Śakas restored the Malwa and the first lady of the empire Dhruvasvāminī, as the lord Viṣṇu appeared in the form of Nṛvarāha to salve the earth from deluge. The land of Malwa and the Dhruvasvāminī is personified as a tiny figure of Bhūdevī seated on the shoulder of Nṛvarāha.

The historicity of Ramagupta is established by the discovery of three Jain idols from Durjanpur bearing upon the inscriptions mentioning the name of Ramagupta as a ruler of Vidiśā of Gupta dynasty. It is also supported by the discovery of copper coins bearing the name of Rāma, written in Gupta Brāhmi. The Ramagupta was of dubious character and weak king offering his own wife Dhruvadevī to the Śaka rulers to solicit his release from Śaka prison. This disgraceful incident is very well narrated in the Sanskrit play Devī-Chandraguptam.[18] The Nāṭyadarpaṇa gives the scanty references. Harṣacaritam of Bāṇa refers to this incident saying that Chandragupta impersonated for Dhruvasvāminī and broke into the Śaka ruler's tent and slaughtered him. It is very beautifully narrated as "*Aripure ca parakalatra-kāmukam kāminīveśaguptaḥ Chandraguptaḥ Śakapatimaśātayata*". The commentator Śaṅkara writing the commentary on Harṣacaritam makes mention of this incident. The Kāvyamīmāṃsā of Rājaśekhara, the Śṛṅgāraprakāśa of Bhoja Paramāra, composed this incident in poetry which was sung by the ladies in praise of the king.

The artistic manifestation of the barren rocky walls of the rock cut cellars at Udaigiri into the miraculous sculptures, carving out of Buddha images at Sanchi and transforming the social endeavour in the stone through sculptures at various places in the district are the unhindered artistic activities that the Gupta patronised.

Vidiśā adorated the multifarious glory under the Gupta where unparallel poetry, drama and the literature were composed fountaining the embellished imaginations.

The Kalachuris who grew to power in north and western Maharashtra, Gujarat and the Malwa during the later half of the 6th century A.D. became the ruler of Vidiśā. The Kalachuri epigraphs speak about the grants and donations made by the ruler at Vidiśā and Ujjain. Śaṅkaragaṇa who ascended the throne after Kṛṣṇarāja and was succeeded by his son Budharāja in A.D. 608 issued a grant from Vidiśā in order to grant the land in Nāsik district. Probably the east Malwa with the Vidiśā as capital was conquered by one of these kings from the last Gupta ruler, Devagupta. The tremendous deluge floaten away the entire city of Besnagar sometime in 7th century A.D.[19] deserting the side and population had to transfer southward for the separate settlement and it is thus the modern city of Vidiśā founded. An inscription from Vidiśā engraved in the reign of Kṛṣṇa (must be the Rāṣtrakūṭa King Krishna III of A.D. 939-68) refers about a magnificent temple of Bhilla-Svāmi an alias name of Sun God popularly worshipped by Hindu community. Sameway an another inscription dated to Vikram Samvat 935 (A.D. 878) mentions the same temple of Bhillasvāmi of Vidiśā. The Ṭabaqat-i-Nasiri refers about the destruction of this temple in 1232-34 probably by Iltutmish.[20]

The political history onwards is shrouded in mystery as we have very scanty evidences but for we have the Chālūkya, Gurjar-Pratihāra, Chandella who seem to have swayed upto Vidiśā for a very short time.

Again Vidiśā and its vicinity rose to prominency under the Paramāra. Siyak II founded an independent kingdom with the Vidiśā on the eastern boundary. Muñja Vākpatirāja extended the territory until he is defeated and killed by the Telap II in A.D. 993. Sindhurāja recaptured the loosen land and his son Bhojadeva illustrious among the Paramāras ruled over the land for more than half century. Someśvara II of the Chālūkya dynasty defeated Jaisingha occupying the Malwa but they had to vacate it for Udayāditya (A.D. 1080-86). He extended the eastern territory of the empire upto the Vidiśā and erected the Nīlakaṇṭheśvara Temple at Udaipur—a marvellous and monumental creation of art of the time.[21] Due to occasional wars between Paramāra and Chandella and Chālūkya this region could not gain the stability and had to swing in the different hands.

REFERENCES

1. (a) Discovery of Lower Palaeolithic, Middle Palaeolithic and Upper Palaeolithic Gyaraspur—*I.A.R.*, 1963-64, p. 89, and 1959-60, p. 71 and other sites like Khīrvai, Kathuri, Kotha, Kharvai, Gamakar, Godvasa, Betwa valley survey, *I.A.R.*, 1959-60, p. 21.

(b) Discovery of Chalcolithic Culture in the excavation of Vidisha in the year 1910 by Lakey, *J.B. A.S.*, vol. XXIII, pp. 135-46.

— In the year 1913-14 By Dr. D.R. Bhandarkar at Besnagar.

—In the year 1963-64, at Besnagar by Mr. M.D. Khare, *I.A.R.*, 1963-64, pp. 16-17; 1964-65, pp. 17-18; and 1965-66, 1-43-45.

2. (a) Motichandra, *Sarthwah,* p. 24.
   (b) *Suttanipātā* (Pali Text Society, 1913), p. 194.
   (c) *Samanta pāsādikā*, Chapter I, Parakaran, 70 '*Ujjainiyam gachanto Vedis Nagaram Patvi*'.
3. Motichandra, *Sarthwah,* p. 131.
4. Following texts refer about the various names of Vidisha
   —*Rāmāyaṇa*, Uttarakhand Verse - 121,
   —*Mahābhārata,* Ādiparva, Vaṇaparva, Droṇaparva, Karṇaparva, Udyoga Parva, Bhishmaparva.
   —*Garuḍapurāṇa, Mārkaṇḍeyapurāṇa, Skanda purāṇa.*|
   —Mahābodhivaṃśa, Dīpavaṃśa, Samanta pāsādikā.
   —Mālavikāgnimitram, Meghadūtam, Kādambarī.
   —City State Coins, published in the *Journal of Asiatic Society of India*, Vol. XXIII, p. 207.
   —Seminar Papers on the Local Coins of India c. 300 B.C. to 300 A.D. (No. 2).
5. Rhys Davids, *Buddhist India,* p. 103.
6. Dr. R.C. Majumdar in his book *Classical Account of India,* p. 307, refers to *Periplus of Erithrian seas* saying 'Desrin' was famous for ivory.
7. *Meghadūtam* - Pūrvamegha, Verses 25, 26, 27.
   Pāṇḍuchchhāyopavanvṛtayaḥ ketakaiḥ sūchibhi-nn-air-
   nīḍārambhairgṛhabalibhujāmākulagrāmacaityāḥ |
   Tvayyāsanne pariṇataphalaśyāmajambūvanāntāḥ
   Sampatsyante katipayadinasthāyihaṃsā Daśārṇaḥ ||
   Teṣāṃ dikṣu prathitavidiśālakṣaṇāṃ Rājādhānīṃ
   Gatvā sadyaḥ phalamavikalaṃ kāmukatvasya labdhā |
   Tīropāntastanitasubhagaṃ pāsyāsi svādu yasmāt
   Sabhrūbhaṅgaṃ mukhamiva payo Vetravatyā-śchaloṛmī ||
   Nīchairākḥyaṃ girimadhivaśestatra viśrā-mahetost-
   vatsaṁparkātpulakitamiva prauḍhapu-ṣpaiḥ kadambaiḥ |
   Yaḥ paṇyastrīratiparimalodgāribhirnāgarāṇām-
   uddāmāni prathayati Śilāveśmabhiryo vanāni ||

8. Mahavaṃśa, Turner, *Pali Buddhist Annals*, 1938, p. 130.
9. Pargiter, *Purana Texts of the Dynasties of the Kali Age*, p. 31
   '*Puṣyamitra Sataschaś to Bhaviṣyanti Sena Nṛpa*'.
10. Bāṇa, Harṣacaritam, A comprehensive History of India, Vol. II, pp. 102-3.
11. *The Age of Imperial Unity*, p. 99.
12. Trivedi, H.V. *Catalogue of the Coins of the Naga Kings of Padmavati*, Introduction, pp. vi, vii.
13. *Ibid.*, viii. Addendum, Some Unique Coins from Bhilsa, p. x, Plate X.
14. R.C. Majumdar and A.S. Altekar, *The Vakataka Gupta Age*, p. 96.
15. *Fleet, Corpus inscriptionum Indicarum*, Vol. III;
   Dr. Vasudeo Upadhyay, *Gupta Abhilekha*, p. 125.
16. *Ibid.*, p. 143.
17. *Ibid.*, p. 10.
18. There is a riddle about the composition of the play, Devichandraguptam. Dr. Kashiprasad Jayaswal, Dr. A.S. Altekar and Dr. V.V. Mirashi are of the opinion that Vishakhadatta, wrote the Devichandraguptam, Jayaswal, *J.B.O.R.S.* Vol. XVIII, p. 17; Altekar, *J.B.O.R.S.*, Vol. XIV, p. 223; Mirashi, *I.H.Q.*, Vol. XA.
19. Khare, M.D., *Vidisha*, p. 174.
20. *Epigraphia Indica*, Vol. XXX, p. 6, pp. 210-211.
21. *The Struggle for Empire*, p. 68.

III

Art History

All the social organisations have as a background, somewhere, working of a peculiar force and the greatest cohesive impulse ever brought into play amongst human units has been derived from all other forces that have worked and are still working to mould the human destiny, none, certainly is more potent than that the manifestation which we call religion. In all the ancient religions which through a voyage maundering in the george of thinkings, preachings, and propagations have come down to us as present day, we find one claim made that they are supernatural, that their genius is not as it were in the human brain but they have originated somewhere outside of it. A dual theory have been accepted by the scholars of which one is the spirit theory while another is the evolution of the idea of infinite. One believes the beginning with ancestral worship while other says the religion originate with the personification of the powers of the nature. Man wants to keep up the memory of his dead relatives and thinks that they are living even when the body is dissolved. He offers the daily needs in a sense to worship them.

On the basis of ancient Aryan literature a few propagate the nature worship theory. Herein they say the human mind seems to struggle to get a peep behind the senses. The dawn, the evening, the hurricane the stupendous and gigantic forces of the nature, its beauty in popling sounds of moisted wind blowing through the showering greenery, bubbling of streams have exercised the human brains and it aspires to go beyond, to understand something about them. In the struggle they endow these phenomenas with personal attributes giving them soul and body sometime beautiful and sometime transcendent. And this side also has a strong case that has made out that the religion has its origin in the personification of the powers of the nature.

If these two contradictory views can be reconciled on third basis, the real germ of the religion can be traced out, which very clearly is the struggle to transcend the limitation of the senses. Either man goes to seek for the spirits of his ancestors, the spirit of the dead, that is he wants to get a glimpse of what there is after the body is dissolved or he desires to understand the power working behind the stupendous phenomena of nature. Whichever of these, is the case, one thing is certain that he tries to transcend the limitations of the senses. He cannot remain satisfy with his senses. He wants to go beyond.

All these inferential knowledge of experiences, prophets have gone from less to more general and from more general to particular.

Patañjali in his Yoga Aphorism says 'Jāti-deśa-kāla-Vyavahitānāmapyānantaryam, smṛti-saṃskārayo-re-karūpatvāt' (Chapter IV, sūtra 9). "There is consecutiveness in desires, even though separated by species, space and time, there being identification of memory and impression".[1]

The unconscious coordination of past experiences reduced to impression, with present conscious action, become memory, a cause to raise the desire with results. And such reversible impressions on human brains mould the saṃskāras. A result is never different from desire, it is but desire reproduced in another form.

And this psychophilosophy of human brain, together with environment has very mystically played behind the carving out of stony media, giving them variant sizes and shapes, the ripe creation. And thus it is that the art is manifested.

The early Indian art and culture seem to have inspired by both the spirit theory and personification of the powers of nature. The megalithic culture is basically evoked out of spirit theory where we do get the burials of deads with the objects of basic needs. Later on we find this idea transformed to Stūpa where the ashes of the deads are buried under the heaps of the soil. The idea of personification of natural powers lies with the Lokapāla-Dikpāla and all the other divine images. All the eight Dikpālas and Lokapālas, for once had been the paramount deities of Vedic concept represent the main powers of the nature.

The art in Daśārṇa and in particular of Vidiśā and its vicinity is endowed with the Buddhist Stūpas, the Sanchi, Satdhara, the Sonari, Bhojpur Pipariya and Andher wherein, the ashes of Buddha and his disciples, Sāriputta and Mahā-Modagallāna along with the Buddhist monks of Śuṅga period had been preserved. Cunningham emphasises upon Sonari Stūpa for the relic casket of Buddha.

In Mauryan period Sanchi Stūpa was constructed by bricks duly bound by mud mortar. This was surmounted by the Trichchhatra Yaṣṭi in the centre cut out in Chunar sand stone. The Trichchhatra Yaṣṭi in the Sabhāparva of Mahābhārata has been termed as Uchchhrita Chaitya yūpa (*Chaityayūp ivochchharitaḥ*. Sabhāparva 22-20).

Among the other Mauryan relics the monolithic pillar with Lion capital is outstanding. The pillar capital at Sanchi is similar to those of Sarnath and Ramapurwa, showing four lions facing to four directions seated on hind limbs on round disc duly engraved by four pairs of swan. Sir John Marshall considers it as "the finest carving India has yet produced and unsurpassed by anything of its kind in the ancient world." While explaining the logic behind the four lions on the pillar capital V.S. Agrawala says that the grand architect of the idea underlying this capital was Aśoka himself as exemplified by the following three facts of his outlook on the life and administration.[2]

The first fact relates to his close contacts with the masses of people which is realised in his own person and where he finally enlightening them explaining the problems of Dharma and moral life.

The second dominant fact about Aśoka was his paramount position as the emperor of vast empire and his deeds as the supreme head of the secular state and also as the spiritual guide, friend and philosopher of the strongly organised spiritual church of Buddhism.

And about the two facts shared by other kings also before and after him but what was the unique as a force in shaping the policies of Aśoka was his new outlook of Dharma or that the law of moral piety which served as a main spring of his action.

The Yakṣa worship seems to be very popular in Daśārṇa Janapada and the antiquity of which goes back to Vedic period. The Yakṣa have been considered as semi-gods, the attendants of Kubera or the God of wealth. Fergusson is of opinion that Nāga worship and Yakṣa worship were prevalent among the non-Aryans, the Dasyus, who were inhabiting the northern lands of the country at the time of Aryan expedition towards the south.[3] There had been a trend to erect a sanctum for Yakṣa outside the village or town as their main deed is to protect the prosperity of the village. In the later concept Yakṣa have been described as the Lokapāla the protector of the four directions such as Vaiśravaṇa is of north, Dhṛtarāṣṭra of east, Viruḍak of south and Virūpākṣa of west.[4]

Vidiśā has yielded a good number of Yakṣa images. A Yakṣiṇī discovered from Besnagar is now preserved in Indian Museum, Calcutta. A lofty image of Yakṣa Kubera and Yakṣiṇī are in District Museum, Vidiśā and two torsoes of Yakṣa recovered in 1963-65 have also been put up at view. All these Yakṣa sculptures depict the art of 1st and 2nd century B.C and in view of Dr. V.S. Agrawala these are the outcomes of traditional folk art.[5]

The Yakṣas are shaped in simple iconography, standing free, colossal in size with massive muscularity. Two armed holding purse, wearing dhoti hanging upto ankles and fastened with girdle. The hair puff is usually shown tied up with turban while the scarf tied the chest. Among the ornaments the heavy ear rings, heavy torque, necklace, armlets and beaded wrist bands are imposing. Not only Vidiśā but from Padmāvatī (Pawāyā) and other parts of the country the abundance of Yakṣa sculptures pronounce its identical tradition both in iconography and the style of art binding the artist of subsequent periods to regard them as model.

The advent of Śuṅga and Kuṣāṇa period marks the multifarious activities in the field of art and architecture which is evident in the four Toraṇ gates of Sanchi and many other sculptures collected so far. The Sanchi Toraṇ depict the various Jatak stories pronouncing the Buddhist philosophy with a glimpse of culture of the time. The philosophical ideas of Buddhism are displayed in symbolic forms as Buddha himself, while for the rest depiction artist has taken liberty imposing his own folk culture. Though the Vṛkṣikā, or the Śālabhañjikā under the two Toraṇ architraves serve the purpose to support the weight, but the idea seems to have germinated from the miraculous birth of Lord Buddha at Lumbini. The panels of Toraṇ-dvār also show the skill of sculptor giving an idea of depth of carving human heads in successive three tiers in which the human heads of lower tier are larger than the middle and upper ones. Same way giving shapes to the houses in the panel they are at diagonal surface to the rectangular panel. The central focal point of the theme is focusing the lines of vision in the panel.

Besides the Buddhism, the Vaiṣṇavism was also essencing the minds of the community. The plan of elliptical Viṣṇu temple unearthed in the Besnagar excavation and Heliodorus pillar inscription clearly indicates the wide acceptance of Bhāgavata cult of Vaiṣṇavism in the area. This inscription records the memorial Garuḍaḍhvaja set up in honour of Vāsudeva by the Greek Ambassador Heliodorus. The fact that he called himself a Bhāgavata, suggests his conversion to the Bhāgavata faith.[6] A few sculptures of Nandī, the bull, have also been picked up and displayed in Vidiśā Museum are the results of experienced artistic efforts with tense muscular development in hump and neck giving a naturalism in the sculpture. In Vidiśā excavations three big altars have also been brought to light with three different shapes as circular, rectangular and Yonikuṇḍa. The traces of two big assembly halls nearby these altars evidently indicate, as Dr. Bhandarkar has expressed, that these mahāmaṇḍapas and Agṇikuṇḍas must have been constructed for the prolonged sacrifices together with religious congregations and preachings.[7]

In the Vedic literature Yajña have been described as medium for the dialogues between the god and the man. It also symbolizes the universal or the cosmic activities with the aim to reduce unconscious to the consciousness. The yajña not only lead the performer to the renunciation, but also connects him with the ultimate goal and this affects upon the entire community. These evidences clearly establish the prevalence of the religious rites in the society in first century B.C in Vidiśā region.

With the Guptas, the iconography started to acquire a definite shape based upon the various norms laid down by the erstwhile Śilpa Śāstras. At the same time the symbolic worship was in transition to the personification as can be witnessed by Ekamukha Śivaliṅga in Udaigiri cave and four Buddha images seated in Padmāsana in the four Toraṇ gates of Sanchi Mahāstūpa. The secularism in art can also be seen in images of Viṣṇu, Umāśaṅkara, Sapta Mātṛkās and various other dispositions of Viṣṇu and Śiva. The Besnagar yielded eight armed Mahiṣāsuramardinī, majestically trampling over the head of buffalo in Samapāda posture now preserved in Gwalior Museum. Among the other noteworthy sculptures from Besnagar and now in Gwalior Museum are the image of Nṛsiṃha a hybrid incarnation of Viṣṇu and the seṿen mother goddesses, one out of these seven has been shifted to National Museum, New Delhi. The sculptures of Udaigiri demonstrate the high ideals of physical charms. Oval face, half folded eyes, broad shoulders, long arms, narrow waist and tappering legs together with the strength in muscularity and the modest ornamentations, draperies and emitting the transparency are the norms through which sculptor has expressed creative delicacy and tenderness of the emotions.

The world famous Nṛvarāha in the cave No. 5 of Udaigiri is a marvellous and a thematic depiction. In comparison to the massive almighty body of Varāha the Bhūdevī, in female personification, is tiny figurine with all the tenderness of feminity. Likewise the river goddess Gaṅgā and Yamunā are shown coming down from the heaven in the female form. They are shown with Pūrṇa Ghaṭa in hands standing on their respective vehicles Kūrma and Makara. The ocean is also given the body of Varuṇa with a pitcher in hand. Varāha rescuing the goddess earth and the other gods including Brahmā, Śiva and the Devagaṇa are praising the act of Varāha. The depiction of Varāha has two basic ideas of which the first is the goddess earth sunk in the ocean and the second is the Viṣṇu who incarnated in the form of Varāha and rescues the earth. The earth goddess is the symbolic representation of the creative power of universe and the principle of motherhood. She is the basic cause for creative nature and to express the unexpressed which is hidden in the deluge. The Varāha is the power rests in the form of Agni, the energy midst the Sun, activate this creative nature, expression of unexpressed and the universal motherhood.[8] We find this idea deep rooted in a hymn of Atharvaveda which says 'this our earths ... ... which in the beginning was water in the sea'. Again the Manusmṛti says *'Iyaṃ bhūmirhi bhūtānāṃ Śāśvatī yonirucyate'* (Manu IX. 37).

'Means the earth the mother of all things and all beings'.

The relation of Varāha, as shown above the symbolic representation of source of energy the Sun God the master of sky, with the earth mother goddess has nicely been described in some of the Rigvedic hymns as '*Dyaurvaḥ pitā pṛthvi* mātā' 'No fancy of nature can be plainer that of 'heaven-father' and the 'earth-mother' are the universal parents'.[9]

Among the other sculptures the Ūrdhvaretas Gaṇeśa and Umā-Maheśvara in the circle, the Nṛsiṃha incarnation of Viṣṇu are noteworthy. There are twenty sculptures of Gupta art preserved and displayed in Gwalior Museum from Vidiśā itself. The endeavour of Jain doctrine can be witnessed by Jain Tīrthaṅkara images in the caves of Udaigiri and the three inscribed Jain images from Durjanpur, during Gupta period.

The Gupta artist undoubtedly was bound by the iconographic principles, but he took liberty in carving the female sculptures giving them fascinating appearance as if he was deeply tempted or to say hypnotised by the unbound miraculous poetic imaginations. Considering Kālidāsa the feminine beauty he described in Meghdūtam (2.21):

> *'Tanvī śyāmā Śikharidaśanā pakvabimbādharoṣṭhī*
> *madhye kṣāmā cakitahariṇiprekṣaṇā nimnanābhiḥ*
> *Śroṇībhārādalasagamanā stokanamrā stanābhyāṃ*
> *Yā tatra syādyuvativiṣaye sṛṣṭiādyeva dhātuḥ'.*

Even the description of Pārvatī's beauteous youthful body has become a characteristic of Gupta-age feminity 'the full breasts pressing against each other without any intervening space between them' and this character is very beautifully marked in the female sculpture but while dealing with motherhood he placed 'taral' (a kind of necklace) between the two breasts.

The ecstasy, the tenderness and the delicacy which moulded the plasticity in the sculptural art during the Gupta period seem to have overpowered by the rigidity in the iconographic disciplines giving the sculptures a super-natural appearance. The development of thinking in religion, philosophy and theology gave birth to several sects controversial in opinion, which tuned up the brain of sculptor to the heavenly prosperity and divinity of Brāhmaṇism. Thus the sculptor engrossed in depicting the cosmic appearance as multi-headed and multi-armed body for the eternal knowledge and to perform the herculean deeds. The tendency of vigorous ornamentation had been the thrusting psychic urges to offer all the worldly property and wealth to the divinity. But at the same time the sculptures of this transition phase reflect the modesty of Gupta age.

We are fortunate enough of having a few outstanding sculptures from the district belonging to this transitory phase. Amongst the Daṇḍadhārī Śiva from Badoh-Pathari, the Śiva playing on the drums, Vīṇadhārī Śiva, the birth of Lord Kṛṣṇa, an incarnation of Lord Viṣṇu, the four headed Brahmā from Besnagar, the four headed Ambika from Gyāraspur, the Yajña-Varāha from Badoh and the Śiva-liṅga can be fingertipped. The Daṇḍadhārī Śiva, of considerably human height, figures the deity, standing in front of bull-vehicle, four armed holding triśūl in one while another is resting on waist. The bull is gazing at the face of his master full of joy and swift smile. The matted hair and Rudrāksa-mālās—the torque are the ornaments expounding the recluse attitude of the lord. The divinity has not transcended the human appearance as the muscular anatomy and the strength in pose points a bridge between the humanity and the super humanity. The hilaric expressions of the rhythm competing the music and melody are finely displayed in the sculptures of Śiva playing on drum. The Śiva has tucked the drum between his cross legs and seems to be very cautious about the thumping of hands. In Nāṭya-śāstra, Śiva has been considered the Lord of music and dance, the originator of that cosmic dance which balanced the forces, that govern the movement of planets. The Badoh sculptures include iconographically a most interesting Śiva-liṅga having the images of Viṣṇu, Sūrya, Brahmā and Pārvatī on four sides. A similar sculpture from Gyāraspur has Viṣṇu, Brahmā, Sūrya and Śiva on four sides evidently speculate the prevalence of panchāyatan worship in the region. The Badoh-Pathari seems to be a centre of Vaiṣṇavism consisting twelve Viṣṇu temples of which only three are standing in a bad state of preservation. Among the ten incarnation of Viṣṇu, Kūrma, Nṛvarāha, Kalkī, Nṛsiṃha, Vāman, Daśarathi-Rāma and Balarāma have been picked up by Mr. M.B. Garde which are at display in the Gwalior Museum.

The domain of art ranging from 300 to 1200 A.D. has been classified into three category, as Dr. V.S. Agrawala suggests, corresponding to three phases of western art, the classical, the Gothic and Rococo conventions as Gupta (300 to 600 A.D.), the early medieval (600 to 900 A.D.) and late medieval periods (900 to 1200 A.D.).[10] As defined by the Kālidāsa, 'Fine Art', 'Lalita Kalā' (Raghuvaṃśa, VIII. 67) reflects indeed a passion of refinement as a patent of every step of life. The elimination of ponderousness and volume and emphasis more and more upon elegance, grace and delicacy are the characteristics of early phase of the art which we find blossoming in the sculptures of late medieval period. The images belonging to late medieval periods and in particular to 9th-10th century, of Vidiśā region denote a wide awareness of synthesis between the external form and internal meaning, a union of speech and thought. The spirituality hidden under the outer form is the writ eloquently in the faces of images combined an intense religious feeling with a tranquil.

The religious activities of various sects such as Śaiva, Śakta, Vaiṣṇava, Buddhist and Jain were aptly centralise in the Vidiśā region and at the same time the Saura-Sampradāya—a sect of Sun worshipper, had also been regarded. A Sun image from Vidiśā displayed in the museum reflects its commandable position on the religious minds of community. The God is shown incorporating by the attendants Daṇḍī and Piṅgala, Ranjyi-Ṛkṣubha. The 'parikar' is showing Uṣā-Pratyūṣā a beauteous personification dawn and evening. These two ladies have been shown with bow and arrow killing the demon of darkness. The surmounting canopy figures the Trinity showing four armed Sun God in the meditation flanked by Brahmā and Śiva. The flying Vidyādhara, Nara and Gaja Śārdūla and worshippers are the decorative motifs. The Sun God is shown with his usual attributes. Among other sculptures the depiction of Kāmadeva with his consort and the lady attendant is eye-catching. The scene is thematic showing Kāmadeva seated under Mango groove on cushioned seat. The consort is embracing Kāmadeva merely by keeping her hand on his shoulder and the lady attendant offering 'soma' in a cup. The joy of union is lustrous on the face. The angularity in body curves, pointed nose, outthrusting lower lip, narrow neck and sharp carving of curly hair give a beauteous appearance to the Kāmadeva considering the demand of theme.

The sculptural art under Paramāra budded many ways, irrespective to the iconographic disciplines several innovations were added with a harmonic vision. The life was wantonous and the luxury was the liking at that time which affected the chisel of sculptor resulting in the images of Nāyaka and Nāyikās. Even the figures of demi-Gods and Goddesses and sometime the deities have aspired with the glimpse of communal environment. The Nāyikā-bheda of Nāṭyaśāstra seems to have gained the popularity. The ornamentation denote the inclination of sculptor to the nature and ecology.

Onwards the first half of 12th century art seems to be diminishing as the body is unbalanced acquiring a cylindrical squat shape with foggy expressions.

A glimpse of early architecture is evident in the reliefs of Sanchi Toraṇ gates showing the pillared motifs. The literary evidences refer about the town planning, house constructions and shrines of these early phases but no traces of them are surviving. The temple architecture begin to acquire a shape by the 5th century; the remains of which are very scanty. Nearby Vidiśā the temple 17 at Sanchi in true sense is the Gupta architecture while to the first cave at Udaigiri the structural maṇḍapa is added. The shrine is carved out in the slope of hill. Cunningham marks it as a first step of Gupta architecture. Though excavations of hilly slopes to form the shrine was diminishing but the Śaiva shrine at Udaigiri excavated by the Minister of Chandragupta II, Vīrasena is the last fair example. Epigraphical records refer about the construction of Sun temple at Vidiśā narrating it as lofty as Kailāśa Mountain.

The mode of alteration and addition and the innovation seems to have begun with the 8th century when the multipurpose ideals of the religion deciminated in the society and a crying need from all corners of the community hummed. Like the composite images a thought was given to composite abode enamouring the tendency of the Hindus to revere all the gods as of equal importance. The Max Müller's Henotheism theory is based for the above idea as it is deeply rooted in Rigvedic hymns which say different gods are considered to be highest gods on different occasions. The epics also narrate the several occasions when the Viṣṇu is praising Rudra or Śiva and vice versa. It is for the spirit of tolerance to consider all the gods of equal ranks, that must have been a basic component to build up the concept of composite figures of abode. The Pratihāra-Paramāra style of architecture seems to have admired this concept and the results are multi-shrine temples. We do find the examples at Hingalajgarh and Kanwala in Mandsaur district and at Bajramaṭh in Gyāraspur in Vidiśā district. Later on this concept got a place of motifs for the decoration in temples as it is clearly visible on architraves of Mālādevī temple at Gyāraspur. The Nīlakaṇṭheśvara temple at Udaipur is the astonishing example of temple architectural style. Profusely studded with the marvellous sculptures relating to the various dispositions of main deity, the temple miraculously have acquired an appearance of heavenly creation. Among the temple plan entrance, Mahāmaṇḍapa and antarāla are added while the facade is equipped with non-functional balconies, as it is seen in the Mālādevī temple of Gyāraspur.

Among the motifs caityagavākṣa, pūrṇaghaṭa, latāvallarī, siṃhamukha or kīrti-mukha are in abundance. The pillars too are constructed with necessary components fundamentally elaborating the height of basement and minimising the height of shaft at places interrupted by the rectangular and circular bands, with inverted lotus, the abacus and the bracket capitals. The shaft is fluted with chain and bell motifs decoration and the four arms of the brackets give space to the Bhāravāhī and Kīcaka. The roof is ornamented with squinch arch designs or a grand lotus which is divided into several rectangular blocks. The spire is almost conical with Amalaksāra and Kalaśa at the top. All the four faces of spire are decorated with vertical bands of Srung and Urusrung in successive tiers.

References

1. For philosophical description see, Rājayoga and Jñānayoga, a compilation of lectures of Swami Vivekānanda, published by Adavaitāśram, Mayavati, Almora, as pocket book edition.
2. Agrawala, V.S., *Studies in Indian Art,* pp. 68-69.
3. Fergusson, J., *Tree and Serpent Worship in Ancient India,* p. 244.
4. Coomaraswamy, A.K., *Yakshas,* pp. 4-6.
5. Agrawala, V.S., *Indian Art,* p. 60.
6. Desai, Kalpana, *Iconography of Vishnu,* pp. 4-5.
7. *A.S.I.R.,* pp. 19-20.
8. Agrawala, V.S., *Yajna Varah, Solar Symbolism of the Boar Incarnation.*
9. *RV.* I. 191.6; *RV.* V. 15.5.
10. Agrawala, V.S., *Studies in Indian Art,* p. 245.

IV

Monuments

Sun Temple : Bajramaṭh
Śiva Temple : Aṭha-Khambā
Viṣṇu Temple : Hindola Toraṇ
Śālabhañjikā : A Celestial nymph
Buddhist Stūpa
Mālādevī Temple

SUN TEMPLE (BAJRAMAṬH)

Situated on the outskirts of the village Gyāraspur by the roadside the Bajramaṭh is a solitary rectangular structure with simple ground plan consisting of Maṇḍapa and shrines, without circumambulation facing to east. The vertical plan is too simple having the pyramidal śikhara crowning the central shrine. The architectural peculiarity lies in three shrines under a roof dedicated to Hindu Trinity – the central one is to Sun God, northern to Viṣṇu and southern to Śiva. Although the temple is in a state of tumbling but the restoration done by the Gwalior State in 1933-34[1] have made it standing. The maṇḍapa is not much decorated except a few pillars having carvings. The roof, too, is a simple stone slab alongwith the simple rectangular pillars at places, seems to be a restoration work. The six rectangular pillars are supporting the tottering roof. Likewise the stones of śikhara are loosely placed and Amalakasār at the top is not properly fitted in the socket. The placement of Jain Tīrthaṅkara image between the śikhara stone to the eastern side obviously indicate to the reconstruction. On the back and southern wall at places a number of stones have been inserted to fill up the gaps with a view to strengthen the wall. Similarly the Jain images placed in all the three rectangular narrow shrines is the work, done prior to 1871-72.[2] These Jain images have created a riddle for right identification till this day. None of the scholars who visited the place identified the temple dedication. Although most of them said it an abode of trinity but they considered Sun God as Brahmā or his replacement as if the word trinity stands only for Brahmā, Viṣṇu and Śiva. They never thought of involvement of Sūrya in trinity which is now established truth by the recoveries of so many composite sculptures of 'Rudra-Bhāskara' and 'Hariharārka'. If we apply the same theory of composite icons to this temple it will be clear that to encompass three shrines under a roof was to solve controversies among three different sects–the Śaivaism, Vaiṣṇavism and Saura-Sampradāya. The epigraphical evidences proved the prevalence of Sun worship in the region during the medieval period as the name of Bhilsa is after a magnificent temple of Bhillasvāmī a disposition of Sun God. Thus to consider the Sun God among the trinity is not unusual. Secondly the main deity of the temple is Sun God while the Viṣṇu and Śiva are subsidiary and this temple must have been built up by Sun worshippers.

The Maṇḍapa was well planned with lateral north and south windows of which the traces of northern windows are visible leaving behind the pillars with round shaft and a few decorations. The windows in fact were the lateral projections of the maṇḍapa. The orientation of the pillars clearly indicate that the original maṇḍapa must be consisting of sixteen pillars of which the four sanctum plasters remain and the rest are the additions.

Looking at the back of main shrines the entire portion is divided into the three parts of which the central one is Pañcarathi in plan, the five decorative vertical bands going top, up to the Śikhara, while the lateral two parts are consisting of three vertical bands and the spire of the both have been dilapidated. Even the debris stones have been removed giving a flat roof to the lateral shrines.

The door frames of the central sanctum are profusely carved out with seven bands of which the first two bands are carved with floral motifs, and Nāga-Puruṣa intertwined forming the loops. The third band depicts the dancers and musicians playing on various musical instruments maintaining a harmony between dance, music and melody. These three bands are emerging from the stone plaques on which the river goddesses Gaṅgā and Yamunā have been carved out alongwith the lady attendants. The fourth band is carved with a chain of four consorts of Sun God Uṣā, Pratyūṣā, Rājyī and Ṛkṣubhā, in dancing posture with bow and arrow. The fifth band depicts four Sun Gods on either side standing in front on the lotus pedestal, two armed, holding full blossomed lotus and putting on ornaments and shoes. The central key figure on the Lalāṭa Biṃba of the lintel is the Sun God seated on chariot driven by seven horses, the head, both the hands and legs from thigh are mutilated. Similarly the faces of the horses are also chopped off and entire body is deteriorated. This Sun God is flanked by Kīrtimukha, Gaja and Siṃha-Śārdūla. The sixth band has given the place to four consorts of Sun God with bow and arrow. The outermost band is a foliage motif with the Kīrtimukha in the centre of lintel. The upper lintel portion has three figures of Sun God in pseudo-niches marked by rectangular pillars. Each Sun God is shown standing on lotus pedestal with a tiny figure of Bhūdevī, flanked by Daṇḍī and Piṅgala and two devotees. The two armed Sun God standing to front is holding fully blossomed lotus in both the hands. There are two lady attendants standing in Tribhaṅga, holding lotus and flanking the outer figures of Sun God while in the central band the Sun God is assisted by the

Cauri bearers. The twelve figures of Sun God or the Dvādaśāditya. Looking at a glance to the central Garbhagṛha, it appears that artist has tried to scoop out the entire Sun God in the form of Prasāda Puruṣa as a spirit of body.

The sanctum is rectangular in size with lofty image of Jain Tīrthaṅkara Ṛṣabhdeva seated in Padmāsana with two elephants and lions at the pedestal and the tiny figure of Gomedh, Yakṣa and Cakreśvarī. This seems to be a later addition.

The central sanctum is separated from the other two by two pillars. The central round and fluted shaft is paralleled by two rectangular bands on either sides. The central shaft has a figure with lady attendant on either side of which the head, breast, hands and legs are mutilated. The rectangular Kīrtimukha are at the middle of shaft and the top is forming the abacus. On the rectangular band floral and creeper motifs have been carved out intertwined with horses and elephants. Both the rear bands have the figures of Nara, Gaja and Siṃha Vyāla. The bracket of the northern pillar has weight-lifter (Bhāravāhī) in the centre and on both the lateral sides in tiny niches Abhisārikās have been figured. One facing to south is the Divābhisārikā Skhalitvasanā with loose under-garment trying to hide her nudity flapping the monkey who is attacking at her. To the south the Nāyikā is standing with a lady attendant holding the purse. She is perhaps be a Gaṇikā, for which the Vidiśa was famous.

The south pillar is quite similar to that of north having Abhisārikā with a child standing at the base of two armed human figure.

The door frame of Northern sanctum has six bands.

The first band having floral motifs. The second has elephants, swans and human figures supported by the wavy loops of creepers. The third one has human figures and design.

At the base of inner two bands the river goddesses Gaṅgā and Yamunā are shown in dvibhaṅga. The fourth band has four figures of Anaṅt-Viṣṇu on both the sides, four armed standing on lotus pedestal in tribhaṅga. Anaṅt-Viṣṇu is crowned with five headed serpent-hood. Similarly the central figure of Viṣṇu at the centre of lintel has given a way leaving behind the bust and the serpent-hood. The outer-most band of door jambs and lintel has a creeper motifs with tiny figures of swan and human in the round loops. The upper part of the lintel has three figures of Viṣṇu in three separate niches with two lady attendants on both the sides and Śaṅkhapuruṣa and Cakrapuruṣa standing by laterally at the base. The Viṣṇu has shown standing in a Sambhaṅga facing front, four armed holding Śaṅkha, Cakra, Gadā and one hand is in Abhaya-mudrā. The twelve figures of Viṣṇu are twelve Keśava as referred by Kāśīkhaṇḍa of Skandapūraṇa.

Similarly southern sanctum is also having six bands at the door frame. The innermost band is having floral design. The second one shows the Nāgapuruṣa, elephants, birds and human figures. Similarly the third one shows the Śivagaṇas in dancing posture alongwith elephants, swans and frog figures. At the base of inner two bands the river goddesses Gaṅgā and Yamunā are shown standing in Tribhaṅga with respective Vāhana—Kachchapa and Makara. The fourth band is maintaining the similarity with the central and northern sanctums bear four figures of Śiva on either side with central figure entirely mutilated on the door jambs. The central figure is flanked by the five figures of Mālādhārī Gandharvas. The Śiva figures are shown standing in Tribhaṅga on lotus pedestal, four armed with lady attendant and vehicle Nandī, holding Triśūla, Sarpa and with one hand in Abhaya-mudrā. The fifth band similarly to that of third, show human dancers and musicians playing on flute, harp and drum. This is associated with swan, elephant and fish figures. The outer band has foliage design with Makaramukha at the centre. Upper most portion of the door jamb shows three standing figures of Śiva in small niches with lady attendants. The middle Śiva figure is totally mutilated. The side figures are, too, profusely chopped out. The bracket of these three figures shows dwarfed Bhāravāhī Makaramukha and lotus pattern. The twelve figures of Śiva are the Dvādaśa-Rudra. The twelve depositions of Rudra-Śiva as we find in Matsya- Śiva- and Viṣṇu- purāṇa. The Śata-Rudra Samhitā also refers about.

All the three outer walls of the three sanctums are occupied by the sculptures belonging to the Aṣṭa- dikpāla, various dispositions of the Śiva such as Naṭarāja, Yogeśvara Śiva, Tripurāntaka, his family members; Gaṇeśa and Kārttikeya, the Viṣṇu images including Nṛsiṃha, Balarāma and Nṛvarāha and the Sapta-mātrikā are also there. Besides the musicians, dancers and nāyikā have also got a fair position. A few sculptures are in niches while others are cut into the stone without any architectural or decorative motifs. The Nāyikās, Sapta-Mātrikās and Aṣṭa Dikpālas are shown standing on bracket pedestals at places decorated with lotus petals, the weather effect has defaced the sculptures and the details of ornaments, decoration and facial expressions are not visible.

The concept of Dikpāla and Lokapāla is very old in Hindu mythology and these are the protectors of four quarters or the directions of the world. Canonically Indra is the lord of East, Varuṇa of West, Kubera of North, Yama of South. The four intercepting directions to these main four directions have been allotted to Agni—southeast, Nṛti—South-west, Vāyu—North-west and Iśana—North-east. But in the earlier texts these stereotype allotment has been interrupted by some other gods. The epic literature groups Sūrya and Caṅdra in the Dikpāla perhaps the insertion of Nṛti and Iśana was not thought of by the time. The Buddhist and Jain texts also differ from one another in characterisation of this group of divinity. The Manusmṛti refers about a king who embodised in himself all the eight Lokapālas, Soma (Caṅdra), Agni, Arka (Sūrya), Anila (Vāyu), Indra, Vittapati (Kubera), Appati (Varuṇa), and Yama. The Gobhilgṛhyasūtra describing the Vastu Śaman mentions the ten offerings (Bali) are to be made to the ten masters of the regions (Diśās).[3] It further includes two more directions and their corresponding masters downwards the Vāsuki and upwards the Brahmā, thus the directions raised to ten.

On the temple walls the Aṣṭa Dikpālas have been carved out and starting from south, clockwisely Indra and Agni, Yama and Vāyu, Kubera and Iśana, Nṛti and Varuṇa are grouped. All the Aṣṭa Dikpālas are four armed and at majority the arms are broken. Indra's thunderbolt and vehicle elephant, Agni's flaming hair, Yama's buffalo, Vāyu's antelope, Kubera's Nakul purse and nṛvāhana, Nṛti's bull are visible and rests of the identifying attributes are mutilated. The Dikpālas have been shown with Karaṇḍa-mukuṭa and ornamented with amiable jewellery.

Considering the central shrine dedicated to lord Sun. The base of central out projected Ratha just above the Adhiṣṭhāna Naṭarāja Śiva has been carved out in a small rathikā. All the eight arms of Naṭarāja are broken either from palm or from elbow, the legs too are chopped out from the thigh. On the pedestal vāhana Nandī is shown looking at the face of Naṭarāja Śiva which is also broken out. A drum player is at the face and trying to maintain the rhythm between music and melody. To the right of Naṭarāja is a Alasa Nāyikā standing on a bracket pedestal. At the top of this central Rathikā above the Naṭarāja is the figure of Yoga-Nārāyaṇ seated on lotus pedestal in Padmāsana, holding Gadā and stalk of Padma and the two hands are in yoga-mudrā placed on the lap of crossed legs with upward palms. Śaṅkhapuruṣa and Cakrapuruṣa are shown seated in savyalalitāsana.

Both the lateral rathas to the central one have been occupied by the divine figures of which on the left Varāhī is shown dancing, four armed, of which, in lower right hand she is holding fish and in the lower left a pitcher. Both the upper left and right arms and the face is mutilated. Nearby, the dancing feet, buffalo is there, following the iconographical principles laid down by Matsyapurāṇa. The figure on the right ratha cannot be identified because, only the torso is remaining. The outer most lateral Rathas of the central shrine, figures Viṣṇu to the left and Ardhanārīśvara to the right as per their iconography. The back wall of the shrine dedicated to Viṣṇu is three Ratha in plan and in the central band is Sun God, four armed and clockwisely holding mutilated, fully blossomed lotus in upper right and left arms, while the lower left is placed on the head of Daṇdi. Among the flanking ratha to the left is Kaumārī which can be identified by her vehicle Mayūra and rest of the identifying attributes have been chopped out. The right ratha seems to be the restoration work having no carving. On the upper part of the central Ratha is Tripurāntaka, a terrific disposition of lord Śiva. The four armed Śiva is shown in ālidha-mudrā. And by two of his hands he is shooting the arrow. A tiny figure of Tripura is shown flying in the sky, among the other weapons sword and shield is clearly visible. Śiva is tensely looking at the aim to confirm that arrow has strucked at right place, he has not lowered the hand holding the bow and hand through which he had thrusted the string is still at the chest. Śiva is flanked by a pair of lady attendants, to the left and right of this panel a Nāyikā and goddess is carved out. The goddess cannot be identified because no identifying marks are there.

The back of the shrine dedicated to Śiva is similar in plan to the shrine of Viṣṇu but it differs in sculptures. The base of central ratha above the Adhiṣṭhāna moulding shows no sculpture except a decorative motif and thus breaks the symmetry. It is flanked by the Nāyikās and both the outer rathas bear the sculpture of Indrāṇi and Naṭarāja. Indrāṇi can only be identified by her vehicle elephant. The upper surmounting portion has been occupied by Nṛvarāha in the centre and eight armed Naṭarāja to the right while the left side figure is of four armed Balarāma. The Nṛvarāha is carved out according to his usual iconography. The Balarāma is shown standing in Sampāda mudrā holding usual attributes with the canopy of serpenthood. The eight armed dancing Śiva pose to the front and had been identified as Kaṭisama by Dr. Gopi Nath Rao on the authority of Bharata's Nāṭyaśāstra. Vāhana Nandī is shown under the feet gazing the dance of Śiva lifting up his head.

The south lateral wall of the shrine dedicated to Śiva is occupied by the sculpture Sūrya in the centre flanked by two figures of Cāmuṇḍas of which left one is Alakṣmī or Yogeśvarī, four armed in dancing posture, with Upaśmāra Puruṣa shown sprawling on the pedestal. To the right is the another figure of skeletonised Cāmuṇḍa with the scorpion marked on the belly., only the torso remains. The top of the centre ratha figures the Nṛsiṃha killing the demon Hiraṇyākaśyapa.

On the northern outer wall of the shrine dedicated to Viṣṇu the images of Brahmāṇī, Sun God and Kārttikeya are carved out above the adhiṣṭhāna moulding. Out of the sculptures images of Brahmāṇī and Kārttikeya are fascinating with joyful expressions displayed on the face. Though the sculptures are badly eroded causing for the patination due to the consecutive rains, the muscular beauty is eye-catching.

Three headed Brahmāṇī is in dancing pose four armed holding the usual attributes of which the Abhayamudrā and Kalaśa can clearly be identified, the vehicle swan is on pedestal.

The image of Kārttikeya is unique in the sense that it is portraying three faces and eight arms. All the eight arms are chopped out leaving behind no trace of attributes to be identified. The vehicle peacock is accompanied by attendants and worshippers of which a lady attendant is looking at the face of lord. In the absence of attributes it is not possible to name the Kārttikeya but an assumption can be made that this must have been the Subrahmaṇyam form, a popular deity among the Paramāras. A life size deity of Kārttikeya with same iconography has been recovered from Hinglajgarh,

District Mandsaur now preserved in Indore Museum. Four armed pot bellied Gaṇeśa is facing to front in a rathika and is flanked by two lady attendants.

The orientation of the sculpture of Bajramaṭha is not in accordance with the Śilpa-śāstras and seems to be disturbed at the time of repair done somewhere, before 1871-72.

The twelve figure each of Gods Sūrya, Śiva, and Viṣṇu portrayed on the door jambs and lintels of the three successive shrines are the twelve dispositions of their respective gods. On the shrine of Sun are Dvādaśāditya while the twelve Rudras include Dvādaśāditya as a form of Rudra and twelve Viṣṇu as twelve Keśava.

Śatarudrīya Vibhūti includes the Dvādaśāditya as a disposition of Rudra. Same way the Kāśīkhaṇḍa of Skandapurāṇa give the name of twelve Keśavas as—Ādikeśava, Jñāna Keśava, Takhyarya-Keśava, Nārada-Keśava, Prahlāda Keśava, Bhṛgu Keśava, Vāmana Keśava, Hayagrīva-Keśava, Bhiṣama Keśava, Nirvāna Keśava, Tribhuvana Keśava. The twelve Ādityas are Lolārka, Uttārka, Sambāditya, Drupāditya, Vṛddhāditya, Mayurvāditya, Khakolkāditya, Aruṇāditya, Keśavāditya, Vimalāditya, Gaṅgāditya and Yamāditya.

Vidiśā has yielded the very interesting panel now preserved in Gwalior Museum have been identified by Mr. N.P. Joshi as Kāśipaṭṭa on the basis of a verse from Aparaji-prachha depicting the city Varanasi.[4] Four such Kāśhipaṭṭas are preserved, one in Vidiśā Museum, one in Vikram Kirti Mandir, Ujjain and two are in Rani Museum, Jhansi. These panels figure twelve Rudras, Sūryas and Keśavas. It seems that this trend has been followed by the artists in Bajraṁaṭh.

ŚIVA TEMPLE (AṬHA-KHAMBĀ)

The monument midst the village and locally known as Aṭha-khambā must have been a magnificent temple dedicated to Śiva, but the Maṇḍapa, Antarāla and only the door of Garbhagṛha remains are standing on a raised platform accessible through four flights.

The four pillars and the lintels are exclusively carved out among which the Ghāṭa-pallava, Makara-mukha and geometrical patterns are visible on the pillar shaft and four brackets which are in fact the abacus of the pillar. The lintel on both the inner and outer sides are marked with the amorous couples separated through the miniature pillars. The dancers and musicians have been carved out in various moods. The roof has flat stone slabs which is obviously a restoration work done by Gwalior State. Amorous couples are expressed in various moods of union showing the third phase the Kāma, from Dharma, Arṭha, Kāma and Mokṣa theory, necessary to attain the complete renunciation. The Antarāla and Garbhagṛha entrance is separated from Maṇḍapa and Antarāla is covered by a flat roof intertwined in eight squares decorated with lotus medallions.

The Antarāla door is richly carved out with Makara and foliage motifs and the brackets and lintel are connected horizontally by an arch, hanging like a garland with three suspending lotus pendants. Both the ends of this arch are emerging from the Makara-mukha. The lintel is also supported by four armed Kīcaka dwarf in shape with flaming hair. The northern Kīcaka is bearded. It seems that in the form of Kīcaka the sculptor tried to personify the Śiva-gaṇas. Likewise the lintel of Maṇḍapa, the lintel of Antarāla is decorated on both the sides with amorous couples and the lady harpists. The four lady harpists are shown standing on lotus pedestal playing on Makara-mukhī saptatantrī vīṇā. The outer part of the lintel facing to Maṇḍapa bears a few figures of Śaiva-cāryas among which one is worshipping the Śiva-liṅgam. This entire panel may indicate to the Śaiva pantheon prevailed in the region during the times.

The door jambs of sanctum gate bear Śiva-rati-hara figures in the middle of the shaft with Nandī as the vehicle. Both the Pratihāras are four armed standing in Tribhaṅga but the faces, hands and legs are mutilated. These Pratihāras are flanked with two lady figures towards the inner side and the outer side there are chanwri bearers. The central main band of both the pillars show Śiva with his consort Umā. The southern door jamb bears the three successive scenes of Kalyāṇa-Sundara while on northern door jamb the Umā-Maheś-vara are shown standing in Dvibhaṅga and Tribhaṅga in small Rathikās. This main central shaft band of door jambs are laterally paralleled by three bands of which inner one is with creeper design. The second one shows some warriers, musicians and amorous couples. The outer most band is of two persons holding hands of each other and standing one above another. On the lintel the central key figure is of four armed Yogeśvara-Śiva seated in Lalitāsana on Sṭhaṇdil. Out of four arms, in lower right and left arm Śiva is holding rosary and pitcher. The upper two arms are mutilated. On both the rear lintel ends, in the projecting Rathikās Brahmā and Viṣṇu are shown seated on sṭhaṇdil in Savya-lalitāsana. Out of the four arms of Viṣṇu three are mutilated. The fourth has rosary and only the cakra is visible. Brahmā is three headed with Jaṭā-Mukuṭa and his one hand is in Varada-mudrā while another holds pitcher. The central key figure of Yogeśvara-Śiva is flanked by Sapta-mātrikās in dancing mood. From south to north Brāhmāṇī, Vaiṣṇavī, Māheśvarī, Kaumārī, Indrāṇī, Varāhī are dancing with their respective vehicles. Cāmuṇḍa, the seventh is shown standing on the Apasmāra-Puruṣa. The Vīrabhadra is in southern side while Gaṇeśa's position to the northern end is very fascinating. He is showing back to Mātrikās and gazing at dance, turning his head backwardly. His right foot is placed on his usual Vāhana, the rat, slightly lifted up while another is resting on floor. The upper tier of lintel is again a band of lady figures and amorous couples of which a few lady figures are dancing while some are playing on flute. The figures are placed in small Rathikās which are crowned by Śikhara.

All the figures are in balance and moderate anatomy with appropriate jewellery. The total creation may be dated back to 8th-9th century A.D.

VIṢṆU TEMPLE (HINDOLA-TORAṆ)

It is an ornamental entrance gateway and as its name signifies look like the stand of a swing. Toraṇ means a prestigious entrance to a sacred or heavenly abode. Preferably it is a lead to a Brāhmaṇical temple dedicated to Viṣṇu as the incarnations on the pillar shafts indicate. It consists of two pillars, standing on pedestals, carrying two horizontal decorated beams supported on brackets and having two small ornamental arches placed in between the two beams. The ends of the bracket capitals are fashioned with lion and elephant's heads, the former facing outward and the latter inwards. The bracket figures are now almost missing. The famous Gyāraspur lady a bracket figure in two pieces was recovered from the debris of the structure in 1933. A miniature śikhara is set up on the centre of the upper beam. The pillars are four faced with depiction of ten incarnations of Lord Viṣṇu.

At a distance of 40 feet from Hindola Toraṇ there stand four pillars on a plinth having eight feet height. These pillars form a square and appear to be a part of the great hall. The excavations have brought to the view portions of the base of a huge temple. The four pillars are evidently the pillars of Mahāmaṇḍapa of the temple. The discovery of the remains of Viṣṇu and Trimūrti sculptures at site suggest that the temple was dedicated either to Viṣṇu or to Trimūrti. The carved ten incarnations of Lord Viṣṇu on the pillars of Hindola Toraṇ and one of the inscription found here opens with salutation to Jagannātha— Lord of Universe—a name commonly applied to Viṣṇu further confirms that it was a Viṣṇu Temple.

The remains show that it was a huge temple having 150 feet in length, east to west and 85 feet on breadth, north to south. It consisted of a shrine room, a Mahāmaṇḍapa with a main entrance and two side entrances, each having a Toraṇ in front of it.

The temple was facing to east. Hindola Toraṇ belonged to the southern entrance.

The excavations, further, revealed a medallion with an inset of Trimūrti, the lower portion of sculpture of Viṣṇu flanked by attendants, the top of the figure with Viṣṇu carved in the centre and Brahmā and Śiva at the ends, a few miniature ornamental spires, threshold of the door-frame of a shrine and āmala-śilās of Śikhara.

All that shows that it had a cell or Garbhagṛha and a śikhara or spire crowned with a āmala-śilās and decorated with medallions and miniature repetitions of the spire.

From the style of carving on the pillars and on palaeographical grounds it is assignable to the early part of the tenth century. Fortunately a Sanskrit inscription, found in a potter's house, is dated V.S. 1067 (1011 A.D.).

On the four respective faces of both the shafts of the Hindola Toraṇ, the ten incarnations of Viṣṇu have been depicted in small niches. The Matsya and Kūrma, Buddha and Kalkī are combined in one niche and the Kṛṣṇa has been replaced by Balarāma of which the only serpenthood is visible. Entire image is chopped out. The Daśarathi Rāma, Paraśurāma are shown standing in Tribhaṅga and two are putting on the amiable ornaments. The faces are either chopped out or defaced due to weather effect. Above this in small rectangular plaques the lady dancers and drum players are shown. The lintel shows the amorous couples and royal personnel with attendants. The Mañjarī placed at the top of the lintel bears two Viṣṇu incarnations Varāha facing south and Nṛsiṃha facing north. Above the dancer plaques there are three successive bands of Ghaṭa-pallava, Makaramukha and floral design.

The Cār Khambā has four pillars exclusively decorated with petal and foliage designs crowning by the bracket capitals having lion and elephant heads. The four lintels placed on these brackets bear Umā-Maheśvara, Lakṣmī-Narāyaṇa, Lakulish, Ambikā and Gaṇeśa in small pseudo-shrines and other parallel shrines have been occupied by the royal couples in embracing and love making moods. All the niches are by laterally balanced with Nāyikās standing on pedestal in various moods, among which the Śṛṅgārikā, Skhalitavasanā and a few dancers are eye catching. The motherhood is revealing through the mother who is feeding the infant keeping him on her lap.

ŚĀLABHAÑJIKĀ (A CELESTIAL NYMPH)

A synthesis after a tiresome whirling of emotions with a delicate fantacy of moonlit night, nearby the glittering pond, the groove shadows portraying the various forms and producing a winsome miraculous sound of breeze and then evokes a feeling out of such a foggy atmosphere, of a loveliest bale, a celestial nymph thumping the heart in astonishing amusement; one ignorantly asks:

Kā tvaṃ kadaṃbasya vinamya śākhām
ekā"śrame tiṣṭhasi śobhamānā /
dedīpyamānā gniśikheva naktaṃ
vyādhūyamānā pavanena subhrūḥ //
atīva rūpeṇa samanvitā tvaṃ
na cāpyaraṇyeṣu libheṣi kiṃ nu /
devī nu yakṣī yadi dānvī vā
varāpsarā daityavarāṅganā vā //
vapuṣmatī voragarājakanyā
vanecarī vā kṣaṇadācarā strī /
yadeva rājño varuṇasya patnī
yamasya somasya dhaneśvarasya //

(*Mahābhārata,* Vaṇaparva; Chapter 265, Vs. 1. III)[5]

It was some time in 1933, while removing the debris

of a temple ruins in Gyāraspur at Toraṇdvāra a torso was picked up, figuring a lady with amiable ornaments and the pendant of torque swinging; very ignorantly sent to the site collection without much notice. A year ticked by and doing the same job, a lady head picked up and same way sent to the collection. A photo of torso is published in the annual reports.[6] Later on while examining the collection somehow; by chance; the head fitted on the torso and thus the life inspired in the stone. Fateful enough to say, the image was carelessly pronounced as 'a woman' merely giving occasional details and without determining its plasticity of art. It is for Mr. S.K. Dixit, who for the first time tried to name this idol as 'Vṛkṣikā' and merely by publishing a photograph on the back of his catelogue,[7] he did not care even to account for. A limit of tolerance, the fascinating smile of bale arrested the probing sights of art critics and thus the "Śālabhañjikā" appeared.

The Śālabhañjikā has popularly been adopted as a motif in Indian art and literature. Vātsyāyana indicates his familiarity with Śahakārabhañjikā (bending a branch of mango tree) as a kind of popular game of ladies. The ladies of north-east India seems to be over fond of this game as this has clearly been narrated in Jātaka stories. Even the Balakāṇḍa of Vālmīki Rāmāyaṇa speak about the Śāla grooves round the Capital Ayodhyā. In early Śuṅga-Śātavāhana art of Mathurā and Amarāvati this motif has abundantly carved out. This game 'Krīḍā' was renowned as the eastern game of recreation.

In the Hīnayāna philosophy of Buddhism the amazing birth of Buddha has been assessed an auspicious groove. It, later on, gained an excellent position in early art as we have five examples at Nāgarjunīkoṇḍa, where on a stone slab Māyādevī is shown standing cross-legged under a Śāla tree. She is holding the branch of tree by her right arm and a lady bearing chowrie stands towards her right. The four Brahmās bearing in their hands golden cloth, marked with seven footprints, approach the lady and proclaim the birth of Buddha. One more stone slab from Nāgarjunakoṇḍa and a stone fragment from Kauśāmbī, now preserved in National Museum, Allahabad elaborately figure almost similar distinctive features.

In reference to the amazing birth of Lord Buddha under Śāla tree, a trend of Śālabhañjikā Krīḍa had eventually evolved into a special festival of this name. The festival is vividly described in Anāthpiṇḍaka.

In the early art Śālabhañjikā had two meanings, first to commemorate the birth of Siddhārtha and second become a popular and prominent art motif to represent a charming beauty scantily dressed adorned with a broad jewelled girdle round the waist that partly covering her nudity.

When the Śālabhañjikā is placed on the architraves of pillars it is termed as Stambhayoṣit. Kālidāsa in Raghuvaṃśam speak of beautiful damsel elegantly carved out on pillars adoring the Capital of Ayodhyā. Various names have been given to Stambhayoṣits as Dohada, Kandūka Krīḍa, Pakṣī, Niśābhisārikā, Surasundarī, Nṛtyābhinaya, Paribhogadarśinī, Prasādhikā, Snāna-sundarī, Toya-Krīḍā and Vīṇā Sāran. These all forms have popularly been depicted in ancient Indian Art.

By the Maurya-Śuṅga and Śātavāhana age in the art, Śālabhañjikā has been classified as Toraṇ Śālabhañjikā, Stambha-Śālabhañjikā and Chaitya Śālabhañjikā. At

Sanchi Śālabhañjikā, display more elegantly the rustic appearance as Toraṇ Śālabhañjikā, denoting to Yakṣiṇī tradition, her coiffure, lower garment, anklets, girdle, necklace, bracelet and bangles are carved out in details by the sculptor.

The Mahāyāna School in Gupta period could not regard the concept of Hīnayāna School, represented through Śālabhañjikā, the birth of Buddha and dominated with Tathāgatahood as permanent and entirely free from the concept of eternity and non-eternity.

It is also noteworthy that the type of Śālabhañjikā of Śuṅga-Kuṣāṇa age could not find a favourable place in Gupta age as the nudity as a rule was discouraged in it and the aggressive beauty or sensuousness of the foregoing period was restrained by a conscious moral sense.

With these ideals we do find a frequent occurrence of Śālabhañjikā in art as well as in literatures. Harṣacaritam and Kādambarī of Bāṇa, the Viddha-Śālabhañjikā of Rajaśekhar, the Arya-saptasati, the Naisadhīyacaritam evince that Śālabhañjikā motif had considerably changed its form and original meaning. In this phase of Indian history Śālabhañjikā simply cannoted as a statue of charming damsel or at time the Nāyikā or the Goddess of splendour or a dancing beauty of groove.

The Śālabhañjikā of Gyāraspur is a meaningful expression of all these ideas, conveying through her mysterious fascinating smile.[8] Dr. C. Sivaramamurti describes it as "Vṛkṣakā a damsel against a tree so sensitively chiselled by the sculptor, that it is unexcelled in the medieval art. This sculpture indeed one of the greatest masterpieces of all Indian Art".[9]

Moon breasted, Swan waisted with magnificent coiffure and her layers of jewellery, the necklaces playing in pride on the breast excite the envy and recalls the beautious imagination of Kālidāsa.

The Gyāraspur lady sometime appears as a nymph 'Paribhogadarśinī', a lady who is deeply engrossed in amorous feelings, make her up elegently goes to grooves to meet her companion, stands crosslegged and clasping the branch of tree in an imposing pose with inviting smile; a starting moment of union. The hero is no where in existence except in exhilarating fantasies of this damsel only; and thus she appears as Niśābhisārikā proṣita patikā; just waiting for the hero.

Kālidāsa in Raghuvaṃśa portrates the queen, wife of Brihadratha, the last of Raghu dynasty, engrossed in deep amorous feeling, recalling previous night's experiences and the king, a hero, from the hide enjoys the shy expressions of the lady—A nāyikā—Paribhogadarśinī.

Any way these all may be the envy fantasies of a poet, or a spectator, or an art-critic. This damsel has plunged into fountain; but she is mystérious to explain, mysterious to understand, a miracle evoked out of the chisel of the sculptor; Śālabhañjikā is the nectar of Gyāraspur art in Pratihāra period.

BUDDHIST STŪPAS

Seen from a distance of 2 Kilometers down the steep of the hill there are the ruins of a Stūpa which at the most is renovated. In 1871-72 Cunningham visited this site and rightly identified the four Buddha images and the remains of Stūpa.[10] In 1931-32, 35-36 and in 39-40 Mr. M.B. Garde surveyed this site and took note of it.[11] No attention was paid to conservation and restoration of these Buddhist remains upto 1958 when for the first time efforts were made to restore the stūpa by stone coping using the lime mortar as the binding material and thus spoiling the antiquity of the monument. Later on they collected all the four Buddha images and dumped them in a store house at Gyāraspur. It is really unfortunate on part of ancient remains collected so far that they are waiting for a dawn of release. In fact Mr. Garde for the first time noted the details and published them in the annual reports of Gwalior State. Mr. Garde has assigned them to the 9th century A.D. considering a diminishing period for the Buddhism. It was the time when the vestiges of Buddhism were continueing at Sanchi as the Sanchi inscription (842) records the construction of a monastery with some chambers at Botśrīparvat (Sanchi) by a Tuṅga in the reign of King Rudra of Malwa in 9th century A.D. He also enshrined the images of Bodhisatva, Padmapāṇi and Vajrapāṇi.

In fact these stūpas are commemorative because of fact that the ashes of Buddhist monks are buried under them; but no attempts have so far been made to find out the truth. Although the stūpas in Daśārṇa region are associated with Buddhism only but the Vedic and epic literature speak much about them. In Rigveda Sūrya is described as a golden stūpa of Agni, 'Hiraṇyastūpa', 'pile of splendour' of which the cosmos is produced. Prior to the Buddhist tradition the stūpas were associated to the life of a Mahāpuruṣa who had truly become transformed into a 'pile of light', visualization of the great spirit whose body is dissolved. The Buddha with perfect knowledge and being enlighten one (Bhagavān, Samyak-Sambuddha) was truly the object of worship through the symbol of stūpa. The community revered stūpa two ways, one considering it as metaphysical symbol, while another as a visible symbol of great light that once was and whose relics were still enshrined within the heart of stūpa. The hemispherical dome surmounted by harmika or Tricchatrayaṣṭī defined as divine mansion (Deva sadana) a symbol of Mahāpuruṣa.

The large platform of considerable height has been raised and is approachable from the north by means of 18 steps flight. The built up of the hemispherical dome is entirely dilapidated and even the debris has been removed by the local treasure hunters which is local popular belief. Originally the stūpa though having four niches of which facing the east have intact while the rest of the three have been filled up by stone masonry by the A.S.I. persons. The niche has a small platform of which a few stones have been removed. The platform facing to east is intact and the Adhiṣṭhān mouldings are clearly visible. The remaining parts of hemi-spherical dome is restored on an another platform which is circular in shape with rectangular projection by three cardinal points i.e. to east, north and south.

What can be assumed about the original appearance of stūpa is lying in the carved stones in the debris. Originally the stūpa must have been encircled by a railing with vertical beams duly couped by the vaulted stones and a few fragments of which show the carving of fully blossomed lotus. The later part of the pillars are shown the sockets in which the horizontal battens were fitted. The platform down the western niche is evidently a restoration work perhaps done by the A.S.I. persons by placing the undressed stone slabs. Mr. Garde has rightly noticed the niches of the lower part of the dome which is dilapidated causing for the Buddha images to slip down. What remains today is only the renovation and no antiquarian remains are there except the fragments of pillars and cross beams.

The four platforms constructed facing roughly the four cardinal directions are truly the pedestals upon which the four images of Buddha were placed. The images are similar in appearance figuring Buddha seated in Padmāsana. Eastern and northern images are in Dhyāna Mudrā and those on the south and west are in Bhūmisparśa and Dharmacakra pravartanā mudrā. In Dhyāna mudrā both the hands are placed on the lap of cross legs with the upwarded palm while in Bhūmisparśa mudra the fingers are touching the earth. In Dharmacakra pravartanā mudrā both the hands are turned to chest touching the fingers. Each image is flanked by two Bodhisattvas. There is an inscription on the pedestal stating *"Ye dharmā Hetu-prabhavāḥ"* means created for the propagation of Dharma. One can assume that the idols must have been carved out by some doner and donated to the stūpa.

Ranging between the same period of 9th-10th century A.D. like the Dhekinath, to the north of Gyāraspur at a distance of one kilometre there are four dilapidated rectangular platforms built of undressed rubbles suggest the remains of Buddhist stūpa. Slightly away from these ruins an image of Buddha seated in Dhyana-mudrā on a pedestal was located, having folds of a loin cloth flowing down the crossed legs. The figure is carved in high relief and set in an ornamental form. Two Vidyādharas holding garlands are shown on the canopy.

MĀLĀDEVĪ TEMPLE

The Mālādevī temple at Gyāraspur is a miraculous outcome of Pratihāra style of architecture. Having cut into the steep of cliff partly and the southern part peering into the valley is structural giving it an eye-arresting appearance. Likewise the other Pratihāra temples the architectural plan of Mālādevī temple is simple with porch, mahāmandapa and sanctum with covered circumambulation. The sanctum and the northern wing of ambulation is vaultedly rock cut hardly assessable, making one to bent upon knees to come out. Unlikely, the sanctum walls outwards in the ambulation are profusely decorated with tri-rath vertical bands and the inserted niches at the base. The temple is standing on pavement with retaining wall.

At a glance the traces of successive restoration done by the Gwalior State are visible. In the Mahāmaṇḍapa two masonry pillars are added to support the roof. At the same time the floor is also repaired. To divide and balance the weight of sanctum facade an additional lintel is inserted above the main door lintel. This total restoration work is done from 1931-32 to 1934-35.

Identification of this temple had also been a mystery without a trace to the scholar's eye as Cunningham termed it as Buddhist shrine identifying the Jain idols of sanctum as Buddhist.[12] The successive spectators concluded a Hindu abode of some goddess which was converted into the Jain temple. Mr. S.K. Dixit termed this temple as Mālādhārī which cannot be stand for any of the God.[13] It is for Dr. Krishnadeva[14] who correctly identify the tutelary image on the lintel of Mahāmaṇḍapa entrance as the Cakreśvarī the Jain Yakṣiṇī the consort of Gomukha Yakṣa the associates of Jain Ādinātha.

The Ardha-maṇḍapa is supported by four pillars with a rectangular roof having a squinch arch with lotus petal design. The rectangular side on the bracket capitals of the pillars is ornamented by a series of miniature temples of which a few are three shrined with Caitya window motifs. At intervals Nāyikās among the Śṛṅgārikā, Darpaṇadhāriṇi and Veṇu-vādikā are shown. The pillars are profusely carved out by floral design emerging from decorated pots. The base of pillar at all the four sides are decorated with temple motifs. The shaft is fluted emerging from a lotus with chain and bell decoration, couped with Caityamukha band. Above this the abacus too at intervals is decorated with Kīrtimukha and Mālādhārī at the extreme corners. On both the lower sides on the facade there are two small niches with śikhara decorated by Caitya-gavākṣa motifs in successive tiers and above which are the Vātāyana in the form of non-functional balconies. The railing of the balconies are decorated by the pitcher-pattern keeping one above another. The small pillars of the balconies are with four brackets in four directions with a smaller shaft ornated with vase and foliage designs.

The Mahā-manḍapa is accessible through the flight of four steps and the base is constructed by three tier lotus pattern decoration. The Candraśilā has similar pattern with rectangular base and the elephant, makara and flower design. Above the makara on lotus pedestal there are two dwarfed figures. It may perhaps be the indication to the water cosmology (Pātāla Lōka). This is flanked by one pair of devotees seated below on knees with hands in adoration on either sides and lady figure sitting behind the male is holding Kalaśa. Besides these figures the seated lion is also shown. The door jambs are of five decorative bands emerging from a panel showing Gaṅgā and Yamunā standing on their respective vehicles with lady attendants holding Chatra and Cāmara. The two male figure on the either sides are shown standing in Dvibhaṅga facing front. Above the lady attendants of the river goddesses on the lotus brackets tiny figures of Sun god are carved out. These are supported with flying Gandharva couples (yugala). The upper most tier of this panel is carved out by the Mālādhārīs and musicians playing on Mṛdaṅga and other instruments. The corners of this plaque are marked with Nāgapuruṣa with seven headed serpent-hood.

The inner most band is merely a floral decoration while the second one is the Nāgapuruṣa in adoration the tail of these are intertwined forming the loops. Next to this band are the amorous couples in small niches supported by the Bhāravāhī. The next band is an imitation of pillar with the base figuring a pot from which the creeper band is emerging. The top of this is decorated by Makaramukha. Similarly the outer fifth band has the floral creepers emerging from the pot. The lintel is carved out by three round bands with Nāyikās in niches standing in various postures, at the rear ends above this two tiers of miniature shrines motifs have been carved out. These are couped by Makaramukha band. On the Lalāṭa-Biṃba at the centre of lintel eight armed goddess has shown on human vehicle which can clearly be identified to Cakreśvarī, a Jain Yakṣiṇī. Three successive bands of lintel are of floral design, Nāgapuruṣa and Mālādhārī Yugala. The roof is decorated with lotus arch design showing architectural mechanism dividing the four corners by 8, 16, 32 and then the finally concave roof.

The beam facing to the facade of temple in Ardha-maṇḍapa shows two tier of miniature temples of which upper one enshrine two tiny figures of Jain Tīrthaṅkara seated in Padmāsana. The later tier has four miniature temple divided by five pillars bearing upon the figures of lady attendants.

There are eight pillars in the mahā-maṇḍapa of which two divide to small Antarāla. The pillars are similar to those of Ardha-maṇḍapa and the decoration on beams are similar to that of Ardha-maṇḍapa. The arch designed roof is dilapidated and open to first storey of the temple. A colossal image of Jain Tīrthaṅkara is placed on a pedestal with two lions and Cakras in the middle. The Jain Tīrthaṅkara is standing in Kāyotsarga-mudrā with two devotees on either side at the base. The walls of Mahā-maṇḍapa have six niches of which two enshrine the images of Jain Tīrthaṅkaras seated in Padmāsana with crowned canopy.

The door leading to sanctum is evidently the later renovation by placing stones one above another without any binding material. The Candraśilā is mutilated on the decorative brackets and the figures carved out are defaced. To the either side of Candraśilā are the seated lions and monkeys. The door jambs are of five bands of which most of the bands are similar to those of Ardha-maṇḍapa gate. The difference is at the northern side. The outer band depict amorous couples, swans and elephants in the loops of creeper. On the door lintel there are seven tiny figures of Jain Tīrthaṅkara. Rest of the door lintel carving is chopped out. In the sanctum there are three images of Jain Tīrthaṅkara seated in Padmāsana.

One Jain Tīrthaṅkara is standing in Kāyotsarga. The roof of sanctum is rock-cut supported by four decorated pillars. Both the lateral gates leading to circumambulation are decorated with the same bands that of floral designs. There are two tier of miniature temples with Jain Tīrthaṅkara. To the north above the lintel the seven mother goddesses with dancing Gaṇeśa and Vīrabhadra have been scooped out showing the adoption of the Hindu Gods in the Jain Pantheon as the tantrism was overpowering the Jain philosophy. The śikhara of the miniature temple with pillar decorations are flanked by standing figures of Jain Tīrthaṅkara. And this is repeated in upper tier. In the northern alley of circumambulation there is an image of praśaśti goddesses among the Ṣoḍaśa Vidyādevī of Jain Pantheon. In fact this is a goddess of learning, eight armed with a peacock as vehicle. She is shown sitting on sthaṇḍila with two lady attendants. The head and seven hands are mutilated from elbow. By remaining one hand the goddess is holding dagger.

To the lateral side of temple facing to south is profusely decorated with six small empty shrines carved by śikhara. The three main thrust bands are decorated with the Caitya window pattern as that on the other side. There are three Jain Yakṣiṇī i.e. Aṗarājītā, Mahākālī and Ambikā are placed vigorously in Rathikās.

Three Yakṣiṇīs are incorporated by Kandarpa, Nirvāṇī, Mahajmālā and Baladevī. All three are four armed holding their respective attributes and vehicle. Among the Yakṣa, Mātaṅga and Kūbera has got a favourable place. The Kūbera is shown standing facing to front, two armed holding some fruit and nakul purse, crowned with the Kīrtimukuṭa he is wearing a loin skin covering only the thigh. The massive legs, chest and hand portrays him in a rigid appearance recalling Yakṣa concept. He is assisted with attendant. Four armed Mātaṅga Yakṣa with the vehicle elephant is carved out in Rathikā flanked by pillars.

In Jainism the iconography acquires the vividness with the appearance of Jain Śāsana Gods and Goddesses. And during their heydays they adopted the Hindu Gods and Goddesses giving them a lower position of attendant or even vehicle.

Though the Mālādevī temple does not contain a variety of sculptures but those are evident show an equal command on perfection imposing a ripe creativity of the time.

References

1. *Annual Administration Reports of Archaeological Department, Gwalior State*, 1933-34, pp. 3-4.
2. Cunningham, A., *Archaeological Survey Reports*, 1871-72, Vol. VII, p. 90.
3. Banerjea, J.N., *Development of Hindu Iconography*, pp. 519-27.
4. Joshi, N.P., Vidiśā ka Varanasi Patta (Hindi), pp. 153. Published in *Purātan*, Vol. 6, ed. K.K. Chakravarty.
5. *Mahābhārata*, Vaṇaparva Chapter 265, Verses 1-3.
   Who art you that, clasping the branch of the Kadamba tree, shinest all alone in the hermitage, glittering like a flame of fire in the night gently bent by the breeze, Oh! you of fair brows? Endowed with superb charm though art and yet fearest not in the dreadful forest. Art you a Devi, a Yakṣi, a demoness, a charming Apsara or a fair Daitya damsel or the princess - incarnate of a Nāga king or a Vanecarī (A woman forester) or a female friend or spouse of king Varuṇa or wife of Yama, Soma or of Kubera?

6. *Annual Administration report of the Archaeological Department, Gwalior State,* 1932-33, p. 7 and see Plate No. IV (a) Torso of Śālabhañjikā.
7. Dixit, S.K., *A Guide to Gwalior Museum,* 1962.
8. Birdi, D.R., (et. al) *Vidisha through the Ages,* 1990, pp. 15-62.
9. Sivaramamurti, C., *Art of India,* p. 231.
10. Cunningham, A., *Archaeological Survey Report,* 1871-72, Vol. VII, p. 90.
11. *Annual Reports of the Archaeological Department, Gwalior State,* 1932-33, p. 5; 1935-36, pp. 4, 5, 11, 15; 1939-40, p. 12.
12. Cunningham, A., *Archaeological Survey Report,* 1871-72, Vol. VII, p. 90.
13. Dixit, S.K., *Catalogue of Gwalior Museum.*
14. Deva, Dr. Krishna, *Temples of North India,* New Delhi, 1969, p. 26.

V

Résume

The sculptural art of Gyāraspur aesthetically appeals to the modest plasticity of the art developed unhindered in the region under the royal patronage. The Paramāras who ruled over the area for more than 350 years successfully recasted the tranquillity which was required fundamentally for such activities. The Muñja and Bhoja Paramāra who had an equal command on sword and pen composed many treatise formulating certain principles for art and architecture. Similarly the lexicography of the time provided the fair subjects to visualise the themes. The religious beliefs and social trends together with secularism extended the fair opportunity to the artist to start with unbound imaginations. The basic fundamentals artist borrowed in succession through the examples from Mauryan, Śuṅga-Kuṣāṇa and Gupta-Pratihāra art of the region and tempted by the neighbouring art activities under Candella and Kalacurīs. With all this, the local artist burst into the faultless creations inspiriting the sensuality in strong media which reveals the vigorous passion, overpowering lust, deep devotion and loyalty of artist in creation and contribution to the plastic art of India.

The Bajramaṭh, a monumental dedication to Trinity, the Śiva-Viṣṇu with leading Sun God. Hindola Toraṇ and Cārkhambi a Vaiṣṇuvite creation, the Aṭha Khambā to Śiva, and the skyscraping Mālādevī temple, expounding the Jain doctrine, on one hand recall the secular beliefs of society and on the other hand recast the glimpses of social environment, custom and traditions. The sculptures carved out in pseudo-niches on the walls of temples, on base and shaft of pillars, bracket-capitals, doorjambs and lintel and on architraves are related to Gods and Goddesses, semi-Gods, Lokapāla and Dikpālas, attendants, amorous couples, dancers and musicians and Saura-worshippers. Moreover the animal and birds, geometric designs, flower and creepers, medallion, makaramukha and caitya window motifs have got a principal place in decorations. Bracket capitals are oriented with Bhāravāhī dwarf in appearance with squat and bulky body.

The images of Gods and Goddesses are scooped out according to the norms laid down in various books of Śilpaśāstra and in Purāṇas, particularly the Matsya-Purāṇa in Devatā Mūrti Prakaraṇam. Philosophically the Tribhuvana Theory has been adopted by the artist in the total depiction of Gods and Goddesses even if they are isolated. The idea has been transformed merely by indications, such as Pātāla Loka, the lowest one, at the base of image by fully blossomed lotus with pedicle and buds and sometimes accompanied by Nāga couples boasting the water cosmology. Above this is Bhūloka, through worshippers and attendants and sometime with priests, while the heaven is imagined by flying Gandharva couples with garlands and some carrying crown canopy. The image of God either standing or seated have shown as the spirit, the power or the energy of the universe. Multi-armed divines are shown holding their respective weapons and wearing modest ornaments. The modesty and piousity is emitting through the facial expressions as the image is shown in various moods such as meditation with half-folded eyes and seated in Padmāsana or with sweet smile on face showering blessings.

Anatomically the images are balanced with sharp curves in the body with no angularity particularly at elbow, knees and at shoulder turns, and the muscularity can be seen in oval face, long suspending hands, tapering legs, narrow waist, in male broad chest and in female, the out thrusting moon breasts. The transparency is created in draperies through which the muscular thigh and knees are peering alongwith the parallel wavy lines or cross motifs are the decorations on garments.

The movement or action in the body can be seen through swinging pendent suspended through the breasts upto the navel. Only the śālabhañjikā for this can fairly be finger tipped. At the same time the position of hands and legs along with the body turns enforce a swift movement and action. The artist has shown a skill in balancing the weight of the body merely on one leg while another is rested on floor simply by toes and fingers, which is evident in dancing images. The dancing Sapta Mātrikās at Aṭha Khambā, the musicians and dancers shown studded in the loops of creepers in the decorative bands of sanctum doors of Bajramaṭh, the flaunting Śivagaṇas with squat bodies, dwarf in appearance are the sensuous creations where the movement evokes the life in stone. Sometime the action in itself narrates the whole story. The Divābhisārikā-Skha-litavasanā is fascinating example for this. The lady is shown standing under a groove. She is holding her loosen lower garment to hide her nudity and trying to flap the monkey by raising her one hand who is attacking at her. The scene is carved out on bracket capital in pseudo-niche. In the panel, the position of hands and the presence of monkey, are the key for the total narration. The lady being excited of amorous feelings had come to make love at the outskirts of village under a groove. The action is over and her lover has just left the place. While sitting on tree monkey was gazing at the love-making couple and now attacking at lady to repeat the same. The position of the right hand through which the lady is holding her lower garment has caught the moment. Perhaps the lady was busy in adjusting her lower garment unaware of the monkey's presence but his sudden appearance has startled her. Now the lady is in two actions at a time, first to hide her nudity by holding the loosen garment and second to keep away the monkey by flapping. Thus the sculptor has successfully casted the atmosphere merely putting in the movement the total depiction.

The carving of a standing lady, with a lady attendant holding purse, in a niche on the bracket capital of Bajramaṭh reminds the Kālidāsa's narration in Meghadūtam about the prostitution in the rock cut caves at Udaigiri, where he warns the cloud messenger describing the vindicative pray of Gaṇikās, calling the place Nīcaiḥgiri. Herein the panel, the action of lady attendant tells the basic theme of the subject.

Again the position of Gaṇeśa in Sapta Mātrikās panel on the architrave of sanctum door of Aṭha Khambā is also amusing. Breaking the monotony of total depiction the pot bellied Gaṇeśa is showing his back to Mātrikās. His one leg is on the back of rat while another is resting on floor. But he is looking at Mātrikās by turning his head backwards. This particular action of Gaṇeśa incredibly denotes to a child's mischievous psychology, as he usually does before his mother. The sculptor has very vigilantly depicted his own family atmosphere.

To appear beauteous, amiable, modest and appealing is natural psychic urge of human beings, particularly in female which is mystically acting behind the innovation of decorations and ornamentation. Wantonness had fiercely enamoured the minds of society and not only the female but male too plunged into the decorations during medieval period. The hair dressings were prevalent and the Dhammilajaṭābhāra and Alakacūḍaka varieties were popularly adopted. To decorate the head with the scarf or fillet was the main trend among the male. Maintaining the harmony as per the status, the sculptor has shown his inclination to nature and environment and at the same time he was excited by social trends. This is evident in the eye catching varieties of coiffures tiden up with horizontal and vertical bands and the hair puffs are decorated with flowers. This is abundantly met with the Nāyakas-Nāyikās, river goddesses and lady attendant figures, in divine community the coiffures show a variety of jewellery bands.

The divinities and their associates appear with a sheer enamour for ornaments. In ornaments the Mudrikas, Padajālaks, Muktadāma, Urudāṃa, Kaṭisūtra, Mekhalā, Udarband incorporating with Harāvali stansutra, channavir, taral and a variety of ear-rings such as Karṇapūrā, Kuṇḍla, Kanakacapāla, Tātaṇkacakra and avantas have gained a wide admirations in the society. Ekāvali, Muktāvalī, Haraśekhar and Haryasti were the popular luxury in the society. The Paramāra artist has tried to represent all these in adoration to the images.

Through the eye of critic the spontaneous imagination of artist seems to be based on his ripe knowledge about the art techniques, religion and philosophy and his wide awareness to custom and traditions. If we speak of art techniques considering the line of forces, the line of movement, the central focal point and the key figures of the panel or the total depiction, we may very well consider the example of dancing Sapta Mātrikās carved out on the architrave of sanctum door at Aṭha Khambā. In the panel seven mother goddesses are shown dancing accompanied by their respective vehicles in order to the description given in Matsya Purāṇa but taking liberty sculptor figured Vīrabhadra in the central of southern band instead of the rear end but the Gaṇeśa is carved at the extreme northern end. This may appear as the faulty creation at first sight but it is in balance to the Cāmuṇḍā carved out midst the northern panel. The key figure of this architrave is the Yogeśvara Śiva in the centre which is balanced by even sized figures of Brahmā and Viṣṇu on the projecting brackets. All the seven Mātrikās anatomically appear taller than the average height. Similarly at Hindola Toraṇ the depiction of ten incarnations of Viṣṇu on the pillar shafts in small Rathikās boast the artist's knowledge about art techniques. Obviously artist was having only eight faces, four on each pillar, to depict the ten incarnations. Among the ten incarnations as the mythological episodes say the combination of Matsya-Kūrma and Buddha-Kalkī could be made. Following the trend to figure the Matsya and Kūrma in amphibious form he skilfully encompassed both the incarnations giving the proper place in a niche while placing together Buddha and Kalkī in a niche he carved out a tall figure of Buddha covering the entire length from top to bottom leaving a considerable space for horse ridden Kalkī. Again violating the Purāṇic or the Śilpa-śāstra instructions and considering the local trends and sentiments, the sculptor replaced Kṛṣṇa by

Balarāma in the depiction of ten incarnations of Viṣṇu. Both the Kṛṣṇa and Balarāma never acquired the prominent place among the avatāras, nevertheless he is an important among Caturvyūha. According to the trends the worship of Balarāma has been greatly influenced by the Nāga worship as he is considered to be an incarnation of Śeṣa-Nāga. Vidiśā and its vicinity once was enjoyed by the Nāga rulers. There are few scholars of the opinion that the famous Nāgā dynasty which ruled over the extensive lands of Padmāvatī (Pawāyā), Mathurā and Kanchipuram was originated at Vidiśā. Dr. H.V. Trivedi has reported a few coins of Vṛṣa Nāga, picked up from Vidiśā, now preserved in Gwalior Museum, is of the same opinion considering the Vṛṣa Nāga as the originator of the dynasty. Considering this description and local religious sentiments towards Balarāma as the lord of the Nāga Dynasty, the carving of Balarāma among the Daśāvatāra seems to be a benevolent justification done by the indigenous artist.

Not only the iconic art is the ripe creativity of artist's unbound imagination but the magnificent sky scrapping temples are the examples of his strong will power and passion. Belonging to the 8th-9th century Pratihāra temple architecture, the temples of Mālādevī and Bajramaṭh consist of Maṇḍapa and Antarāla. In Bajramaṭh the three shrines are combined under a roof crowned by a pyramidical śikhara with Śṛṅga and Urūśṛṅga. This is a new innovation done by the Pratihāra artist which was later on adopted by the Paramāras, as it is seen in the ruins of Pārvatī Temple at Hinglājgarh Varāha Mandir, Kanvalā in Mandsaur and at Āśāpuri, district Raisen. The idea behind the construction must be the secularism to avoid the controversy among the various sects. The three shrines of Bajramaṭh are dedicated to Sūrya, Viṣṇu and Śiva, in fact a creation of composite Prāsād Puruṣa which later on transformed into the carving of Rudra Bhāskara and Harihārārka images in late 10th century A.D. Moreover, the sanctum doors of all the three sanctums in itself are the body of respective Gods, it is evident from the carving on the door jambs and lintel. The middle shrine is dedicated to Sūrya as the leading God, indicate towards this total erection by the Sun-worshippers. Dr. Gopinath Rao propounds his theory about the composite icons that the central key figures indicates its respective pantheon for its creation. On all the three sanctum doors the respective Gods along with twelve dispositions have been carved out. The Sun God is having Dvādaśāditya along with his attendants Daṇḍī and Piṅgala, his four consorts Uṣā, Pratyuṣā, Ranjyi and Ṛkṣubhā with bow and arrow as if the image of the Sun have been carved out. Similarly the Śiva is accompanied with Dvādaśa-Rudra, his attendants and consorts representing a Śiva image and the same theme is followed on the sanctum door dedicated to the Viṣṇu by carving the twelve forms of Keśava.

Similarly the Mālādevī Temple with some variations show addition of non-functional balconies and the entrance, 'Praveśa', before the entry to the Mahāmaṇḍapā. The Śikhara is pyramidical with Ratha and Urūśṛṅga exclusively decorated with Caitya Gavākṣa motifs and gauze motifs. The sculptures of Jain Śāsana Yakṣa and Yakṣī are studded on the outer wall showing no pattern. This temple is Sandhar—with rock cut circumambulation are decorated as those of outer-walls.

At Aṭha Khambā and Cār Khambā only the pillars and the architraves are the remains and expounds nothing architecturally important.

BIBLIOGRAPHY

Sanskrit Literature

Aparājitapṛchcha, Gaekwad Oriental Series, Baroda, 1960.

Dīpavaṃśa, Turner, Pali Buddhist Annals, 1938.

Garuḍa Purāṇa, Chaukhamba Series, Varanasi.

Mahābhārata, Bhandarkar Oriental Research Institute, Poona, 1927-64.

Mahāvaṃśa, Turner, Pali Buddhist Annals, 1938.

Mārkaṇḍeya Purāṇa, Chaukhamba Series, Varanasi.

Meghadūtam, Kālidāsa Granthavalī, Sitaram Chaturvedi, Kashi V.E. 2001.

Rāmāyaṇa, Bhandarkar Oriental Research Institute, Poona, 1927-64.

Ṛgveda, Vedic Samsodhan Mandala, Poona, 1933-46.

Viṣṇu Purāṇa, Sanskriti Sansthan (Hindi), Barelie, 1971.

Viṣṇudharmottara Purāṇa, Dr: P. Shah (Ed.), Baroda, 1961.

Modern Works

Acharya, P.K., *Hindu Architecture in India and Abroad,* Bhopal, 1979.

Agrawala, V.S., *Bhārtīya Kalā* (Hindi), Varanasi, 1977.

Agrawala, V.S., *Studies in Indian Art,* Varanasi, 1966.

Bāṇa, *Harṣacaritam, A Comprehensive History of India.*

Banerjee, J.N., *The Development of Hindu Iconography,* University of Calcutta, 1956.

Bhattacharya, Chintamani, *Gobhilagṛhyasūtram*, Delhi, 1982.

Birdi, D.R. (et al.), *Vidiśā through the Ages*, Delhi, 1990.

Coomaraswamy, A.K., *Yakshas*, Washington (1928-31).

Cunningham, A., *Bhilsa Topes*, Varanasi, 1966.

Dixit, S.K., *A Guide to Gwalior Museum*, 1962.

Dixit, S.K, *Mother Goddess*, Poona, 1943.

Fergusson, J., *Tree and Serpent Worship in Ancient India*, London, 1868.

Fleet, J.F., *Corpus Inscriptionum Indicarum*, Vol. III, Calcutta, 1888.

Gupta, Parmeshwarilal, *Bhāratīya Vāstu Kalā* (Hindi), Varanasi, 1979.

Joshi, N.P., *Prācīn Bhāratīya Mūrti Vijñāna* (Hindi), Patna, 1977.

Khare, M.D., *Vidiśā* (Hindi), Bhopal, 1985.

Krishna Nanditha, *The Art and Iconography of Vishnu-Narayana*, Bombay, 1980.

Majumdar, R.C. (Ed.), *Classical Accounts of India*, Calcutta, 1960.

Majumdar, R.C. & Altekar, A.S., *The Vākāṭaka Gupta Age*, Delhi, 1960.

Marshall, Sir John H., *A Guide to Sanchi*, Calcutta, 1918.

Minhaj-ud-din, *Tabaqat-i-Nisiri*, Tr. by Major H.G. Raverty, London, 1881.

Mirashi, V.V., *Satavāhanon aur Paścimī Kṣatrapon kā Itihās aur Abhilekh* (Hindi), Lucknow, 1982.

Moti Chand (Dr.), *Sārthwāh* (Hindi), Patna, 1953.

Munshi, K.M., *The Struggle for Empire*.

Pargitar, F.E. (Ed.), *Dynasties of the Kali Age*, London, 1913.

Patil, D.R., *Cultural Heritage of Madhya Bharat,* Gwalior, 1952.

Percy Brown, *Indian Architecture,* Bombay, 1971.

Ray, Krishan Das, *Bhāratīya Mūrti Kalā* (Hindi), Varanasi, S. 2030.

Roy, U.N., *Śālabhañjikā,* Allahabad, 1979.

Sharma, Dr. R.K., *Madhya Pradesh me Purātatva ka Sandarbh Granth* (Hindi), Bhopal, 1974.

Sivaramamurti, C., *The Art of India,* New York, 1977.

Sompura, P.S., *Bhāratīya Śilpa Saṃhitā* (Hindi), Bombay, 1975.

Tiwari, Dr. M.N., *Jain Pratima Vijñān* (Hindi), Varanasi, 1961.

Trivedi, Dr. H.V., *Catalogue of the Coins of the Nāga Kings of Padmāvatī,* Gwalior, 1957.

Trivedi, Dr. H.V., *Kālidāsa Varṇit Madhya Pradesh Caturdhām,* Vikram Samvat 2015.

Thakore, S.R., *Catalogue of Sculptures in the Archaeological Museum,* Gwalior-Lashkar.

Upadhyay, Vasudev, *Gupta Abhilekh* (Hindi), Patna, 1974.

Upadhyay, Vasudev, *Prācīn Bhāratīya Stūpa, Guha and Mandir,* Patna, 1972.

Journal and Reports

Annual Administrative Reports of the Archaeological Department, Gwalior State, 1923-40.

Archaeological Survey, Vol. XXIII, 1910.

Archaeological Survey Reports, 1871-72.

District Gazetteer, Vidiśā, 1979.

Epigraphia Indica, Vol. III & XXX.

Imperial Gazetteer of India, Vol. VIII.

Indian Archaeology - A Review, 1950, 60, 63, 64, 65 & 66.

Indian Historical Quarterly, Calcutta.

Journal of Asiatic Society of India, Calcutta, Vol. III.

Journal of the Bihar and Orissa Research Society, Vol. XVIII & XIV.

Marg, Vol. XXVI, No. 3, Bombay, 1973.

Purātan, Vol. VI, Bhopal, 1989.

INDEX

LIST OF ILLUSTRATIONS

PLANS

PLATES

16. General view : Mālādevī Temple
17. Southern view : Mālādevī Temple - Showing non-functional balconies and pseudo-shrines, and innovation in the architectural style of Pratihār art.
18. Ghaṭa-pallava motif on pillar shaft : Mālādevī Temple
19. Details of architrave and roof showing pseudo-shrine motif and lotus medallion : Mālādevī Temple.
20. Kubera : A Jain Yakṣa
21. Panel showing river goddess : Mālādevī Temple
22. Goddess Mansa : A Jain Yakṣī

Plans

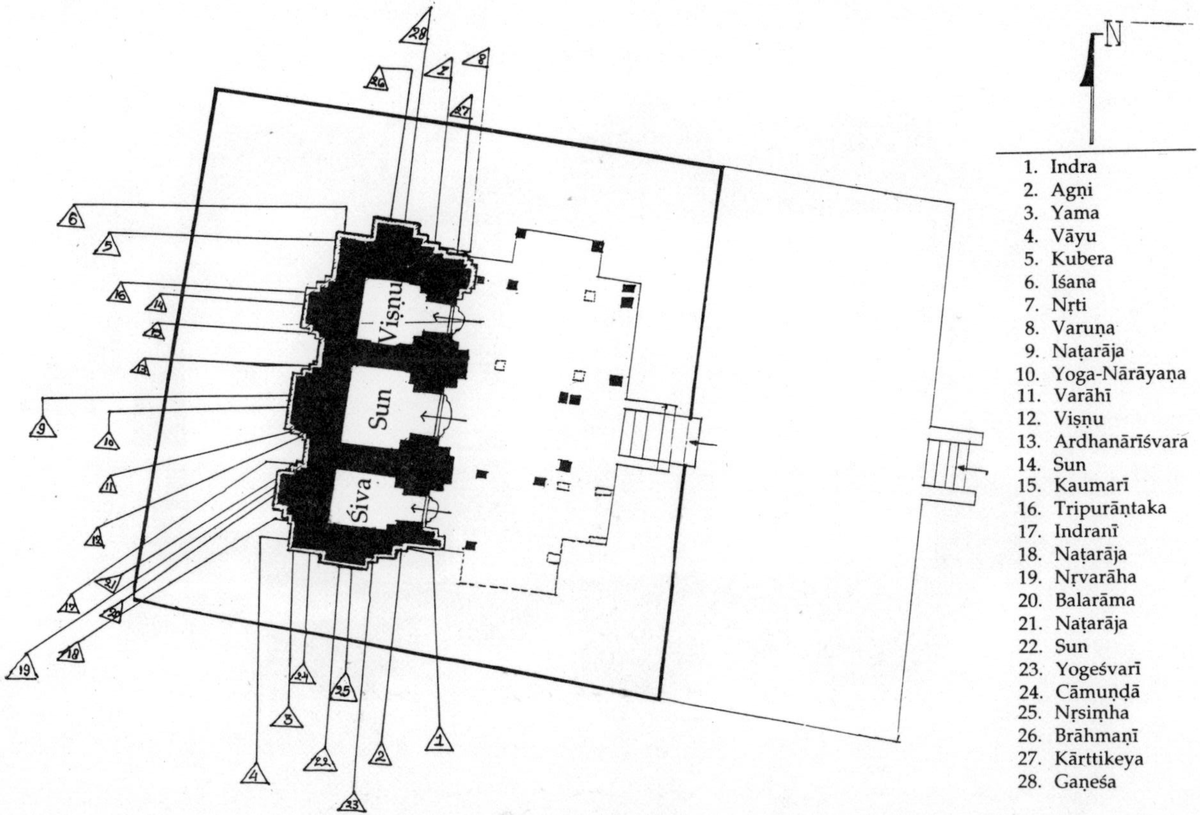

1. Indra
2. Agṇi
3. Yama
4. Vāyu
5. Kubera
6. Iśana
7. Nṛti
8. Varuṇa
9. Naṭarāja
10. Yoga-Nārāyaṇa
11. Varāhī
12. Viṣṇu
13. Ardhanārīśvara
14. Sun
15. Kaumarī
16. Tripurāṇtaka
17. Indranī
18. Naṭarāja
19. Nṛvarāha
20. Balarāma
21. Naṭarāja
22. Sun
23. Yogeśvarī
24. Cāmuṇḍā
25. Nṛsiṃha
26. Brāhmaṇī
27. Kārttikeya
28. Gaṇeśa

1. Plan of Bajramaṭh, Gyāraspur showing position of Sculptures

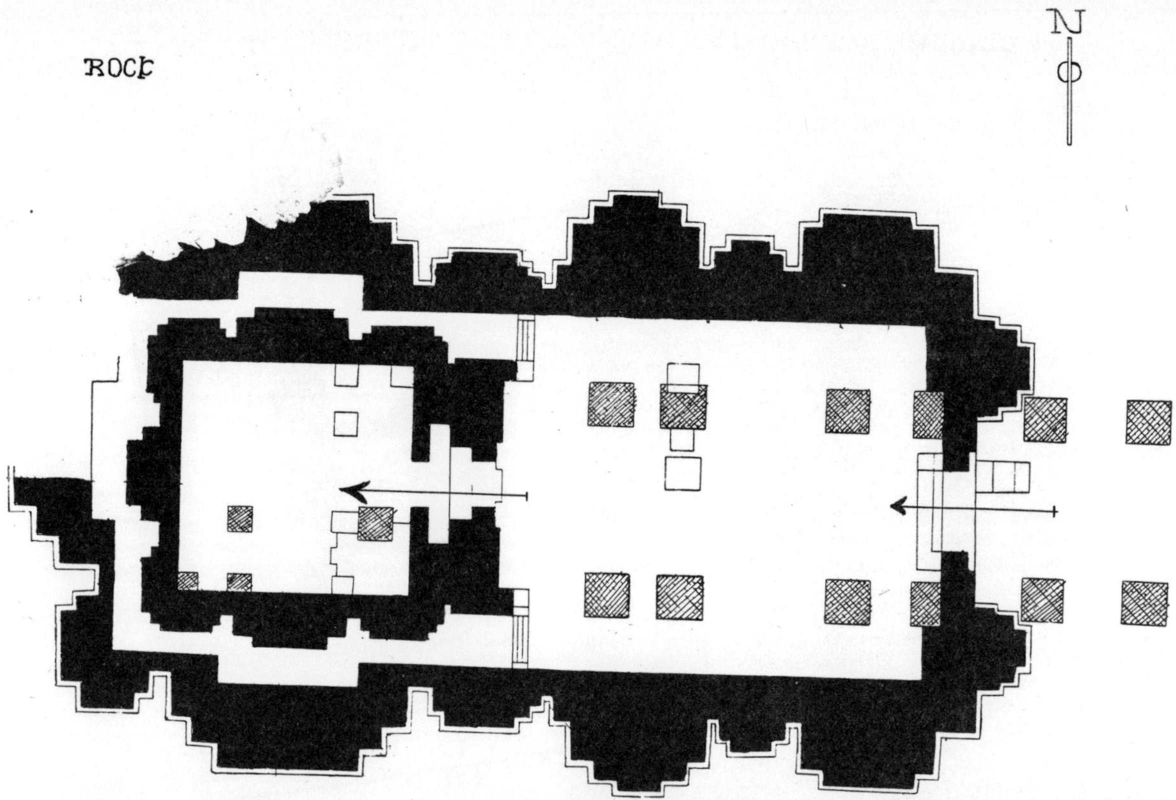

2. Plan of Mālādevī Temple

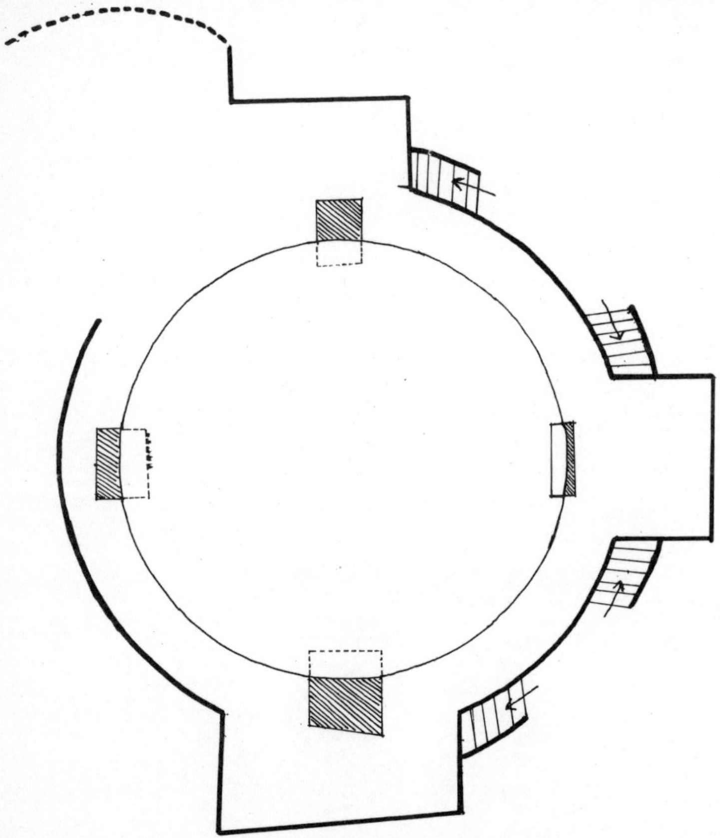

Plan

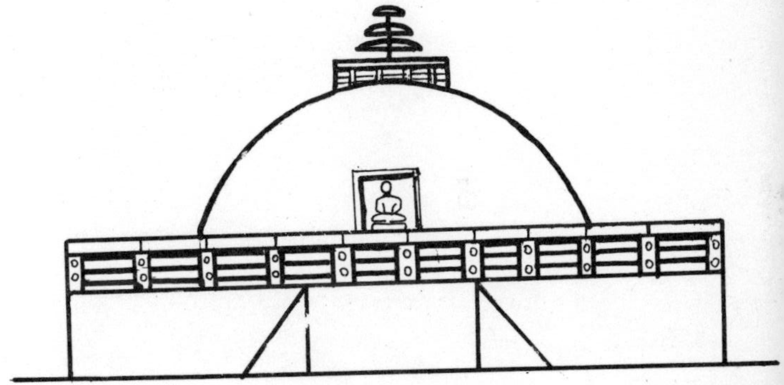

Conjectural Diagram

STŪPA DHEKINATHA

Plates

Pl. 1

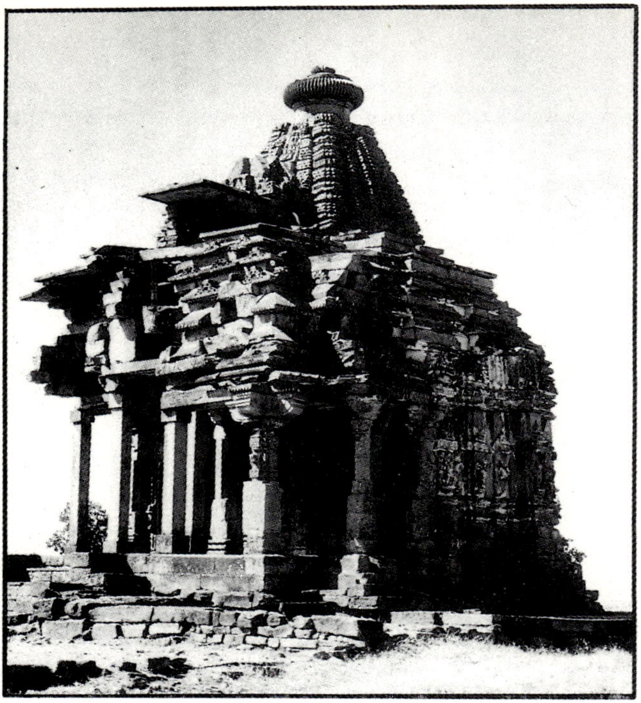

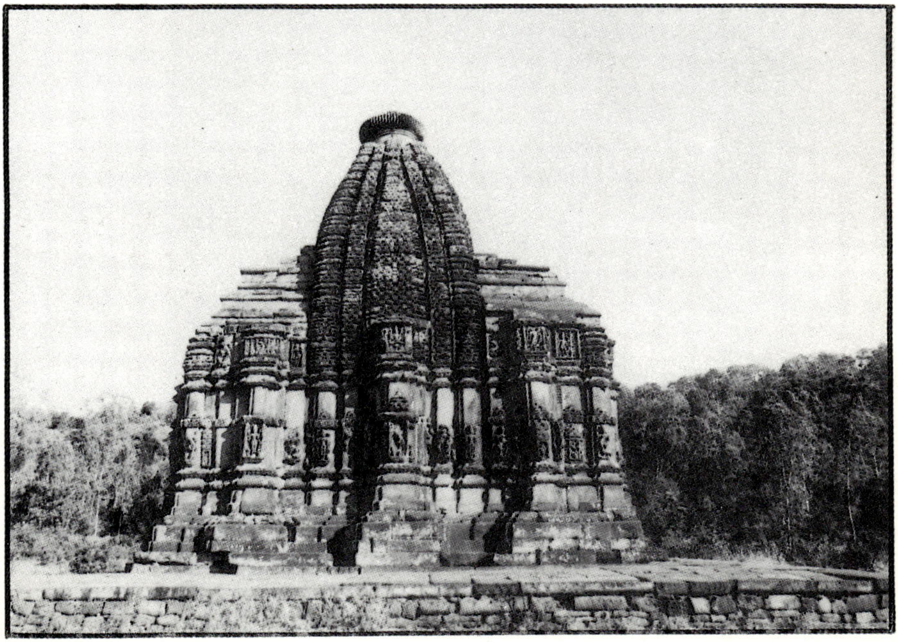

Pl. 2

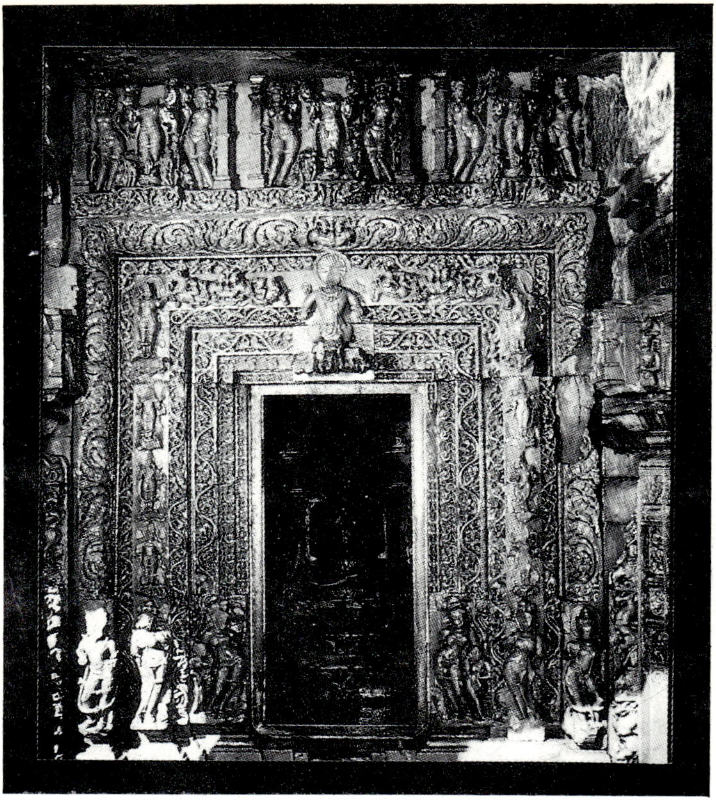

Pl. 3

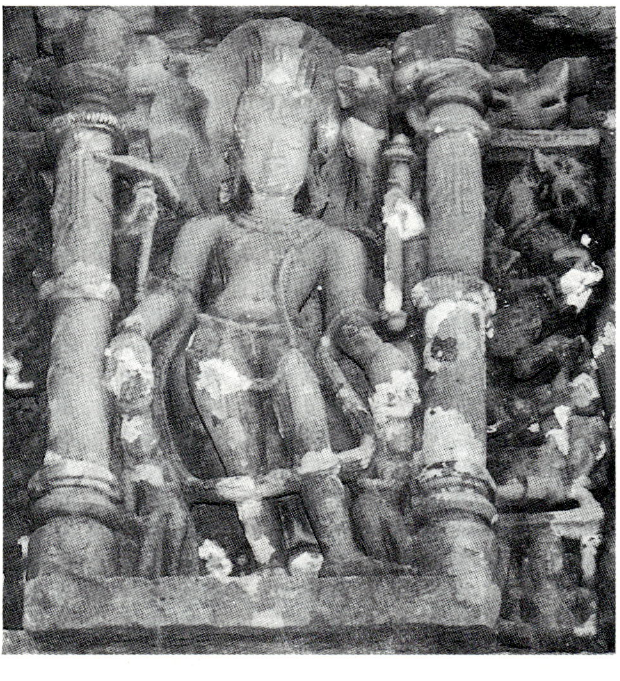

Pl. 4

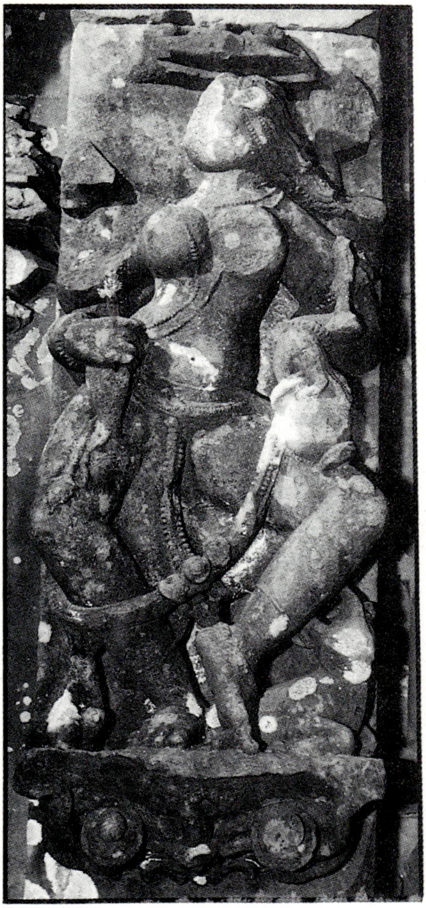

Pl. 5

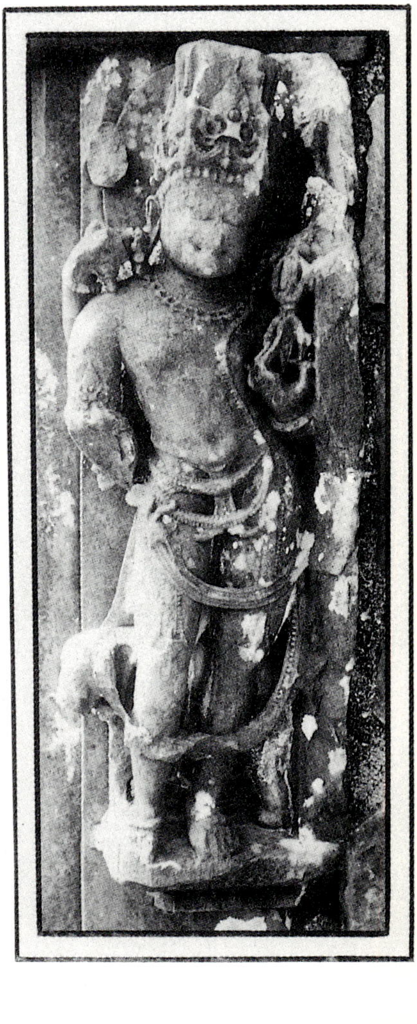

Pl. 7

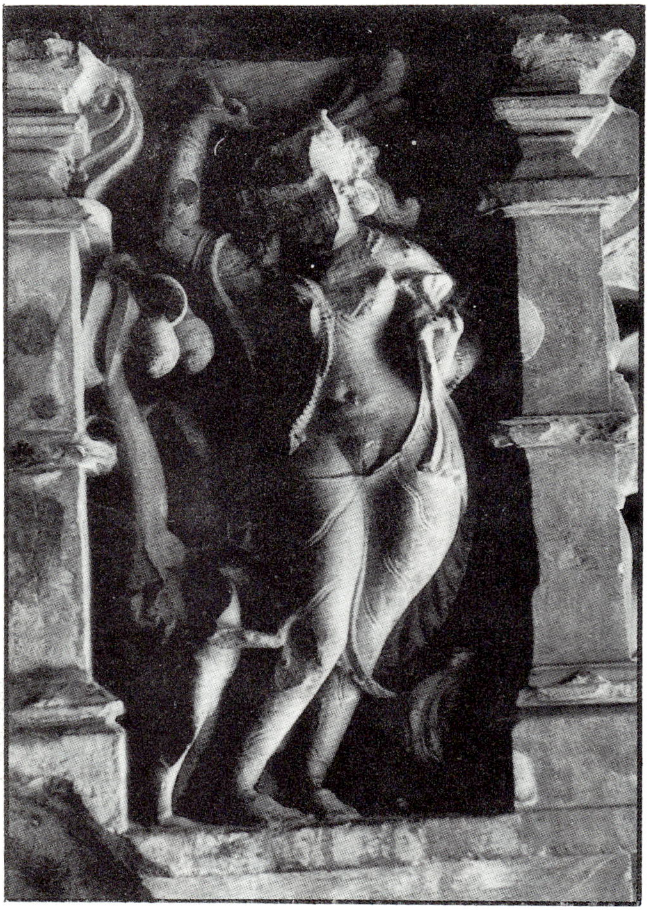

Pl. 6

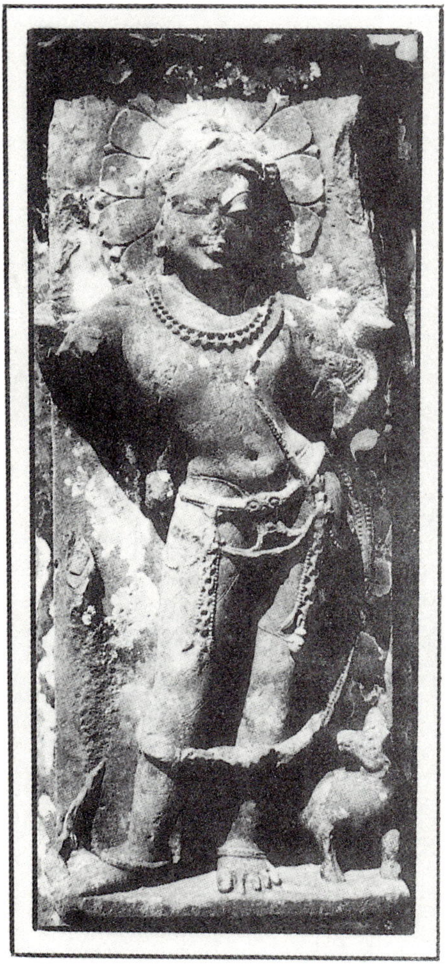

Pl. 8

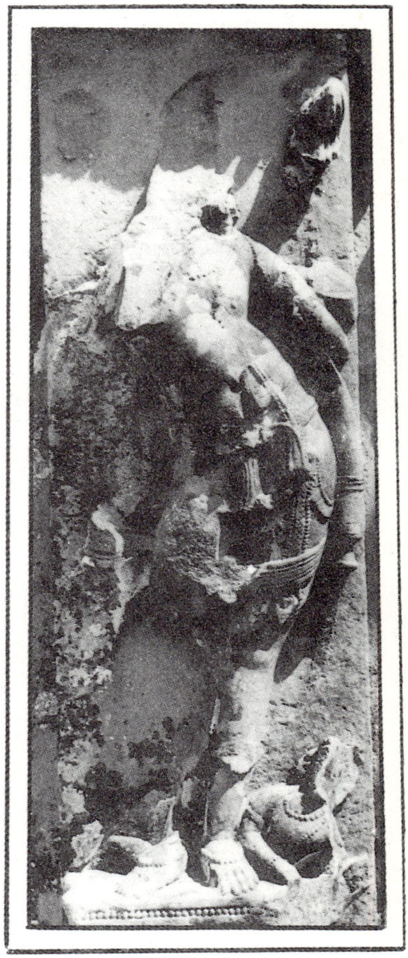

Pl. 9

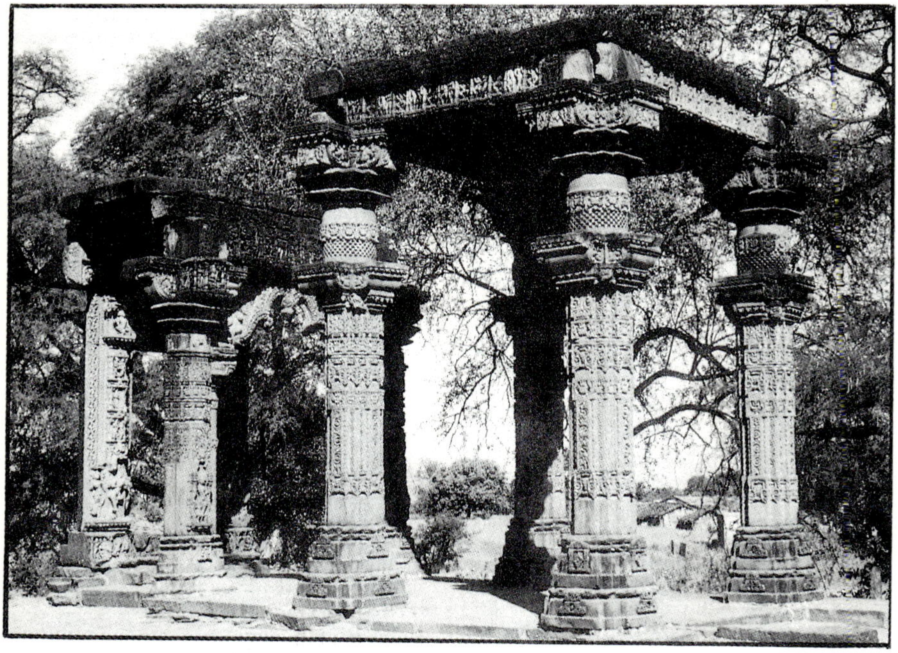

Pl. 10

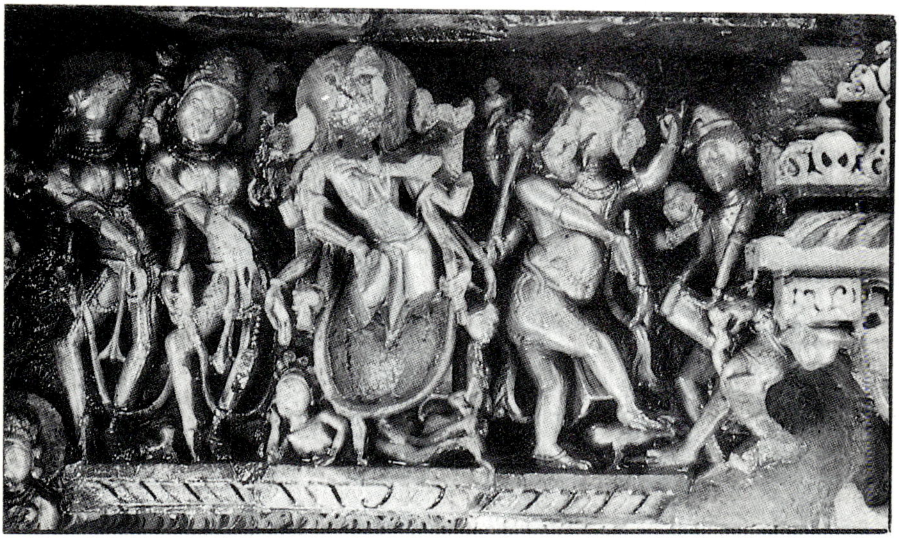

Pl. 12

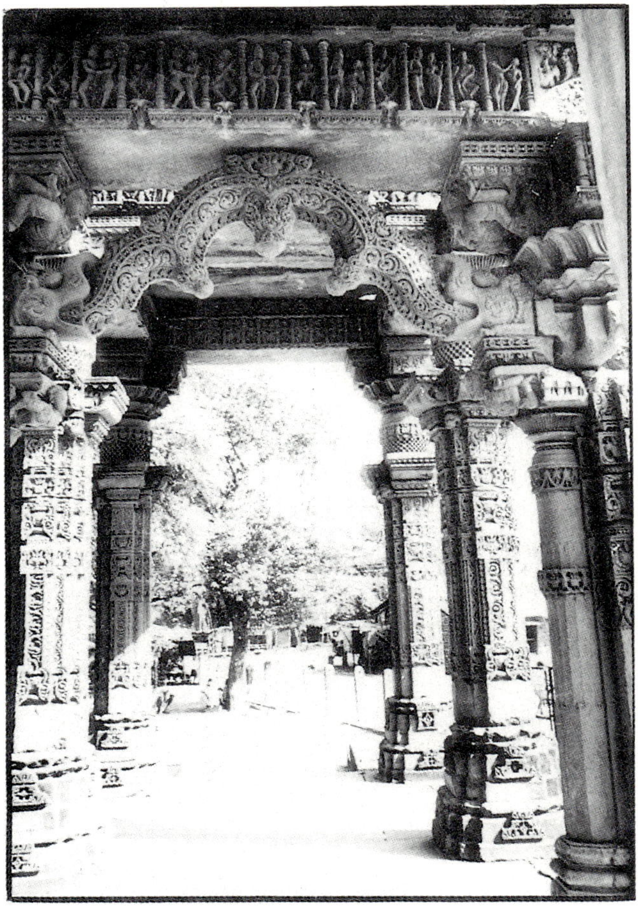

Pl. 11

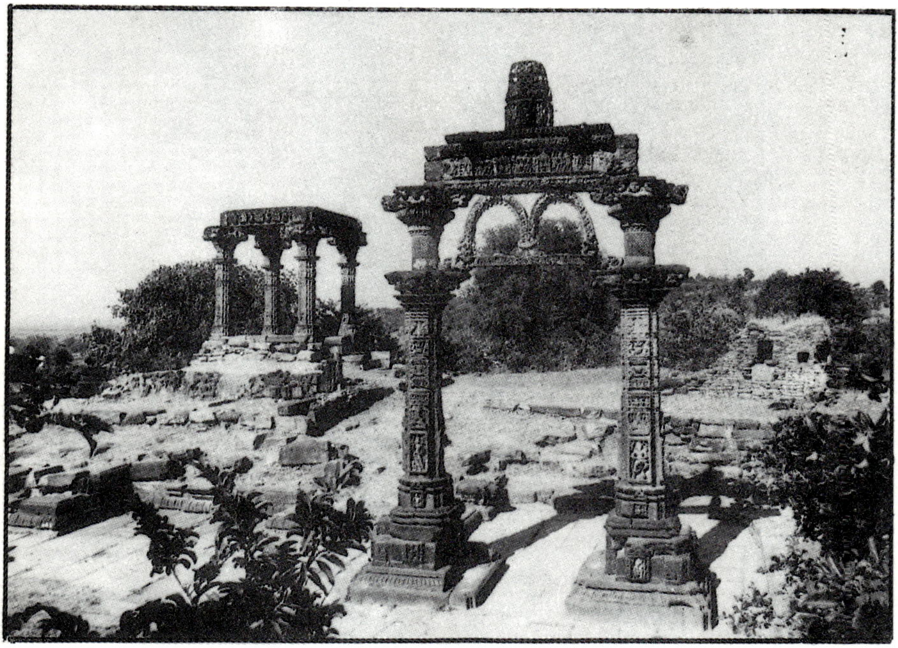

Pl. 13

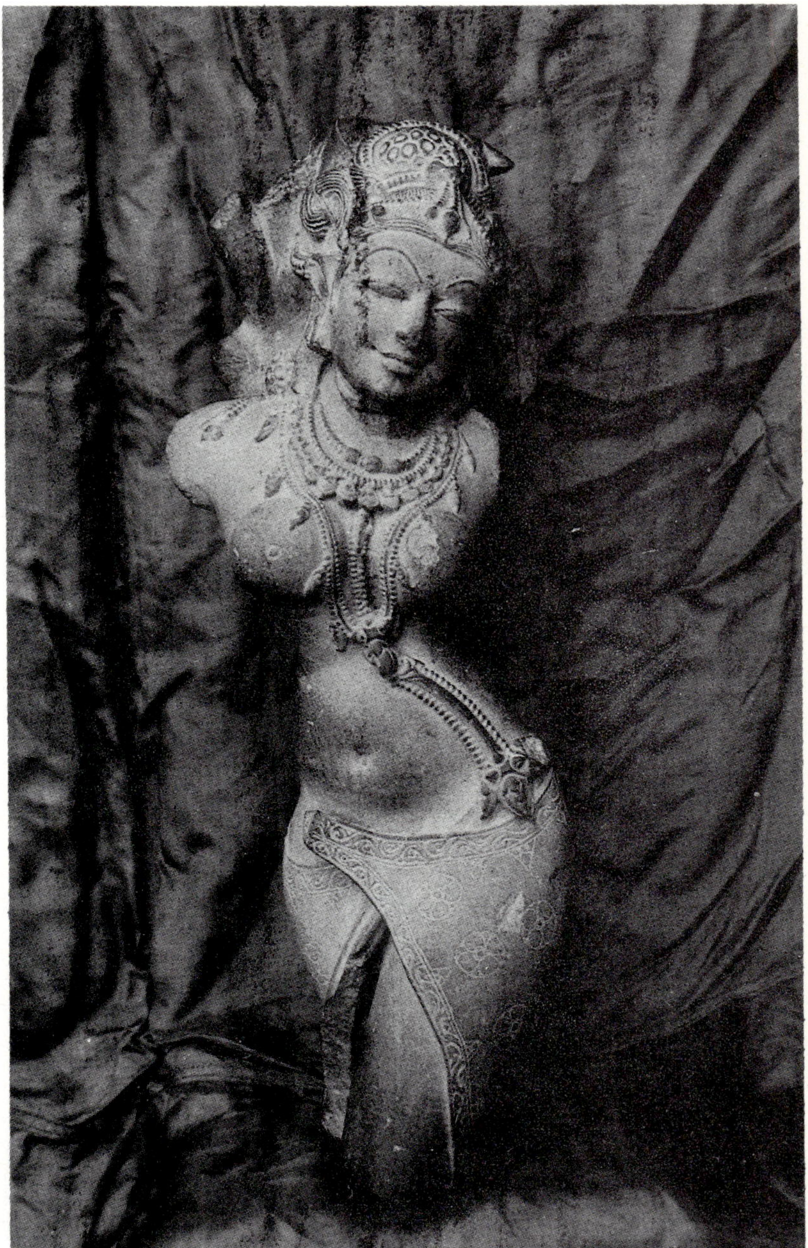

Pl. 14

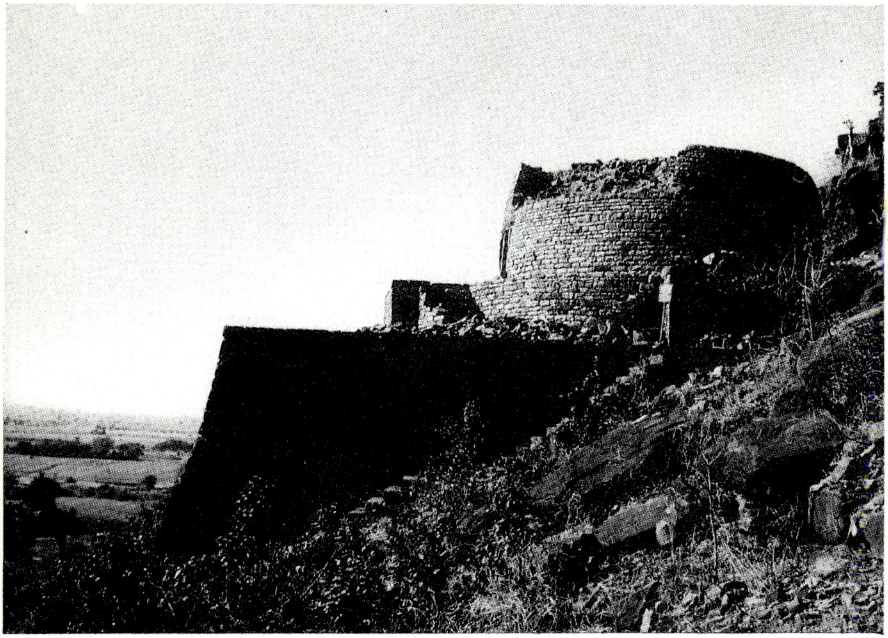

Pl. 15

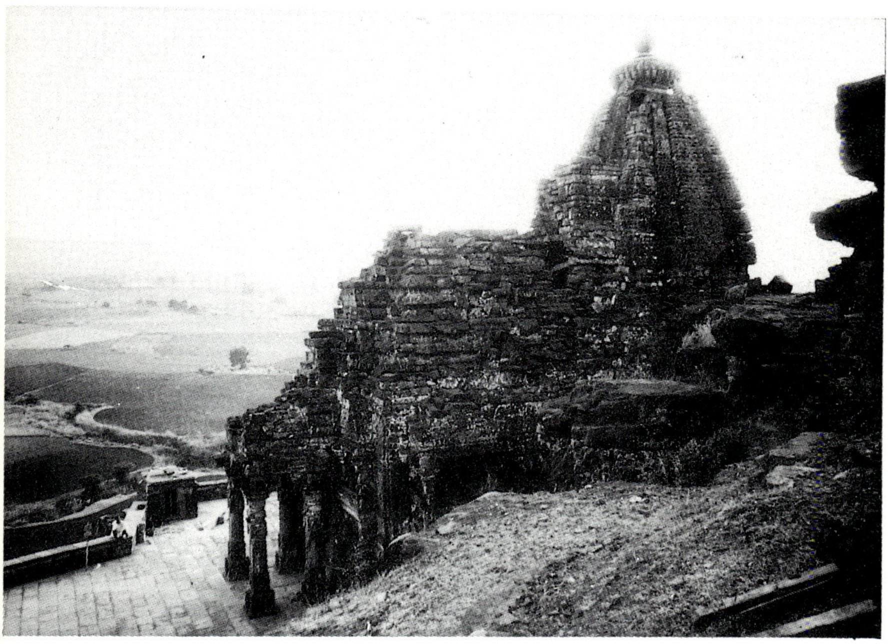

Pl. 16

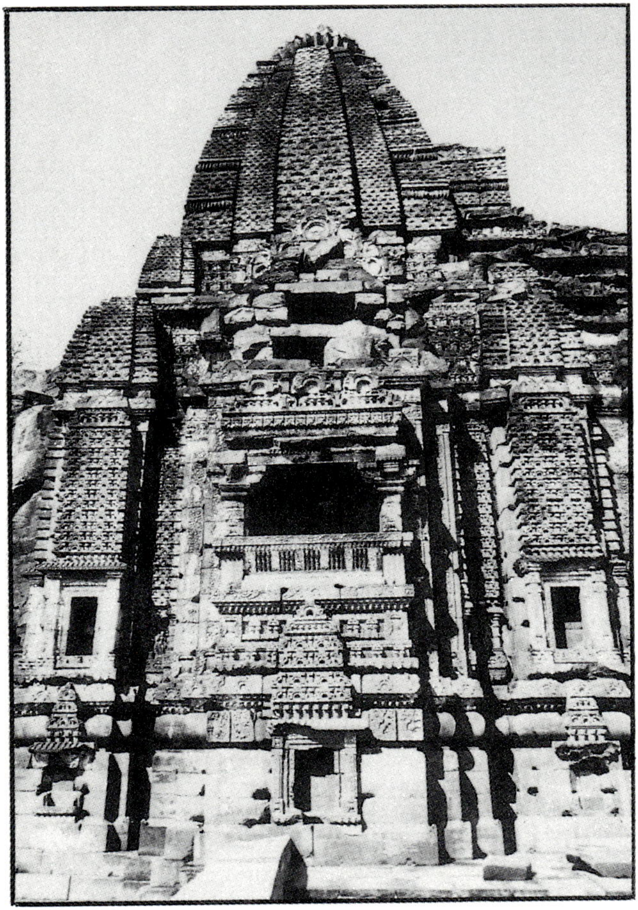

Pl. 17

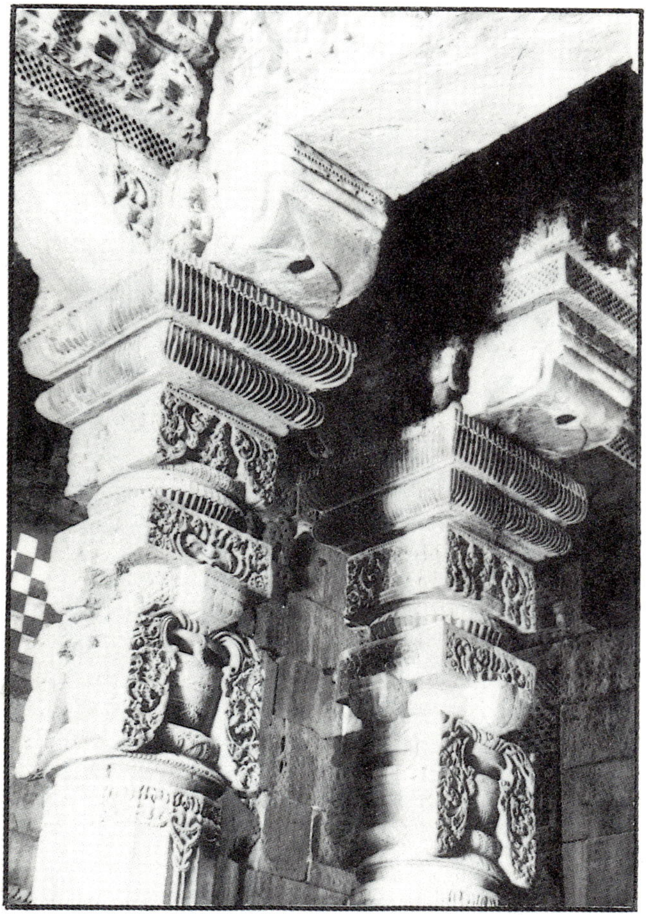

Pl. 18

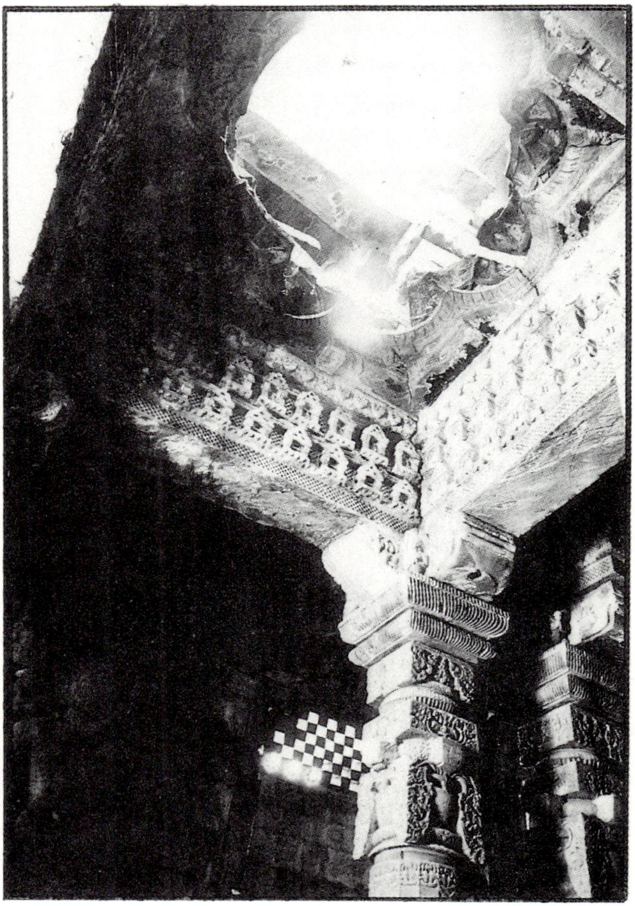

Pl. 19

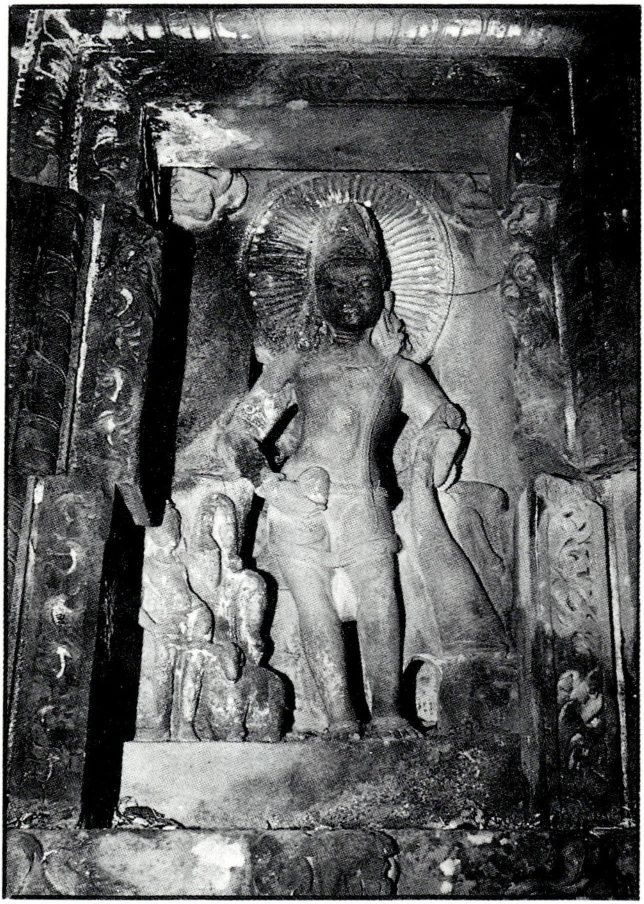

Pl. 20

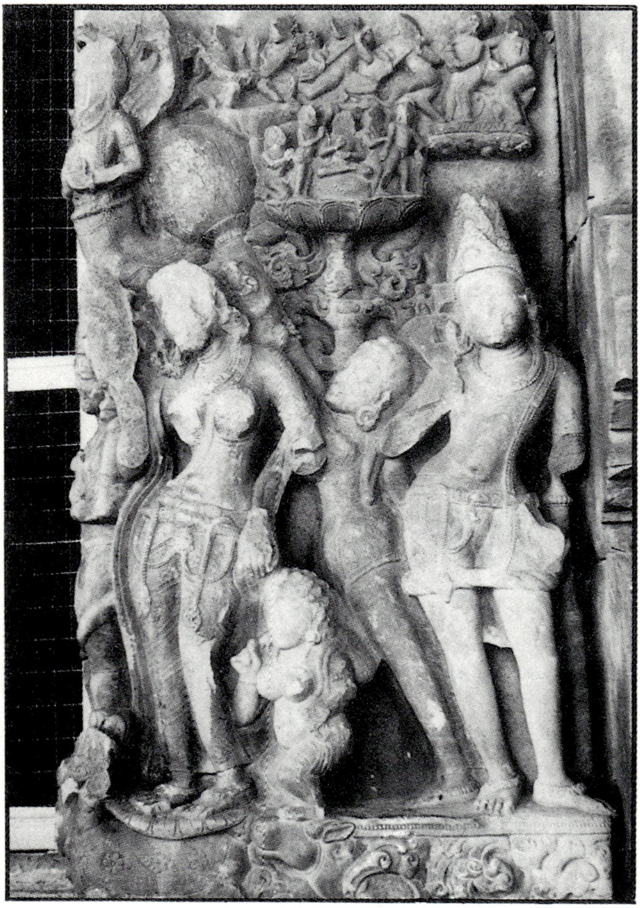

Pl. 21

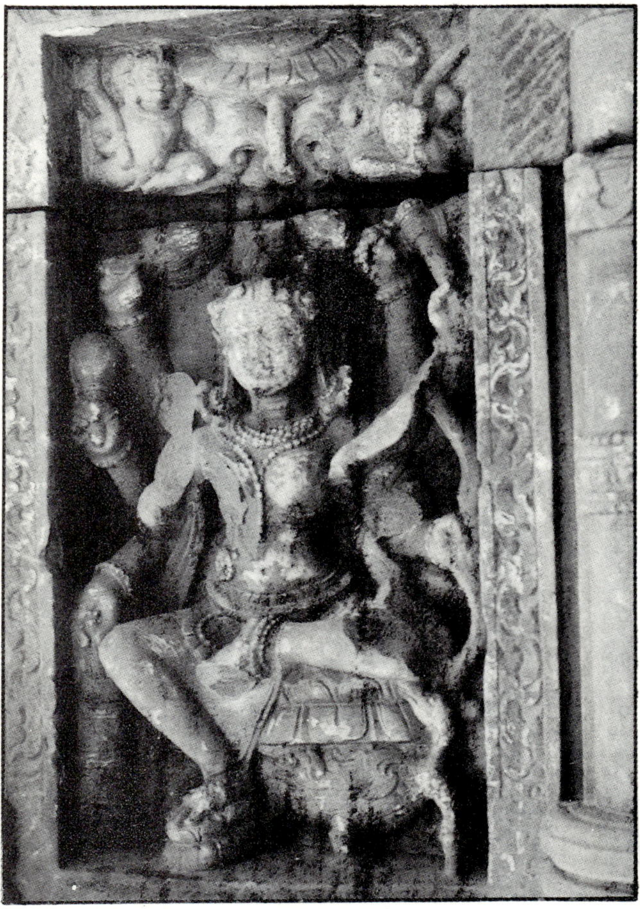

Pl. 22

120